Jesus

J F Aylett *and*
R D Holden-Storey

Hodder & Stoughton
A MEMBER OF THE HODDER HEADLINE GROUP

Acknowledgements

The authors would like to thank the following for their assistance with visual research:

Liz Aylett; Terry Barringer, Deputy Librarian of the Royal Commonwealth Society; the United Society for the Propagation of the Gospel; the Friends of Vellore; the National Gallery of Jamaica.

The Publishers would like to thank the following for permission to reproduce copyright material:

The Bible Society/Collins for the material from *The Good News Bible;* Lutterworth Press for extracts from The Infancy Story of Thomas in *New Testament Apocrypha* (1963); Methuen for extracts from *The Secret Diary of Adrian Mole* (1983); and Hodder and Stoughton (Publishers) for extracts from *The Hiding Place* (1971) and *More Than Tongues Can Tell* (1982).

Every effort has been made to trace copyright holders of material produced in this book. Any rights not acknowledged here will be acknowledged in subsequent printings if notice is given to the publisher.

The publishers would like to thank the following for permission to reproduce copyright photographs:

Mohamed Ansar, p. 57; Barnaby's Picture Library, pp. 24 (right), 38, 40, 59 (right), 60 (left); Biblioteca Apostolica Vaticana, p. 8; British Film Archive, p. 26; British Museum, p. 6; The British Society for the Turin Shroud, p. 56; Casa dello Scugnizzi, p. 29; China Christian Council, p. 46 (right); C. M. Dixon, p. 47; Friends of Vellore, p. 43; Ny Carlsberg Glyptothek, p. 9; Sonia Halliday Photographs, pp. 24 (left), 28; Sonia Halliday and Laura Lushington, p. 60; Robert Harding Picture Library, p. 18 (right); Daisy Hayes, pp. 27 (left), 46 (left); Hodder & Stoughton, pp. 60 (right), 61; The Kobal Collection, p. 7 (right); Abbas/Magnum, p. 51; The Mansell Collection, p. 55 (right); MCOD, p. 18 (left); Monastere Benedictin de Keur Moussa, p. 54 (top right); Fiona Moorman, p. 52 (left); National Film Archive, p. 7 (left); The National Gallery, p. 50; Zev Radovan, p. 27 (right); Rex Features, pp. 4, 5, 7 (middle), 35, 41, 48 (left); John Ryland's University Library of Manchester, p. 11; SCALA, p. 30; Ronald Sheridan's Photo-Library, p. 16; Jamie Simson, pp. 32 (both), 52 (right), 59 (left); Dr. Patricia Smith, Hebrew University, p. 53; "The Society for the Propagation of the Gospel", pp. 37, 48 (right); Spectrum Colour Library, p. 54 (bottom right); The Post Office, p. 21; Rainbird Picture Library, p. 40; Colin Standing, p. 54 (left); Tate Gallery, p. 22; United Synagogue Publications Ltd, p. 23; USPG Photo Library, p. 55 (left); Jerry Wooldridge Photolibrary, p. 45; Zefa Picture Library (UK) Ltd, p. 39.

Cover photograph: All Saints Church, Tudely, Kent by kind permission of Dr S Coles.

Every effort has been made to contact copyright holders of material in this book. Any rights not acknowledged here will be acknowledged in subsequent printings if notice is given to the publisher.

British Library Cataloguing in Publication Data

Aylett, J.F. (John F.)
   Jesus.
   1. Jesus Christ
   I. Title II. Holden-Storey, R.D. III.
   Series
   232
ISBN 0 340 49050 0

First published 1990
Impression number   20 19 18 17 16 15 14
Year   2005, 2004, 2003,

Copyright © 1990 J F Aylett

Typeset in 12 on 13pt Plantin Roman by Taurus Graphics, Abingdon, Oxon.
Printed in Dubai for Hodder & Stoughton Educational, a division of Hodder Headline Ltd 338 Euston Road, London NW1 3BH

Authors' Notes

Events before the birth of Jesus are given as BCE (Before the Common, or Christian, era); dates after Jesus' birth are given as CE (Common, or Christian, era).

Words in bold **like this** are explained in the glossary on page 63.

Contents

1 Who is Jesus?

Every ten years, the people of a small German village put on a play. It is always the same one and they have been acting it for over 300 years. It is about the last few days in the life of one man.

He was a carpenter's son who lived about 2000 years ago. He was not a rich man; he did not lead large armies or control great empires. Yet he became one of the most famous people who ever lived. His name was Jesus.

During his lifetime, a few hundred people in Palestine became his followers. Often, they did not understand what he taught them. Yet, after his death, they began to tell others about him. Today, many millions of people all over the world **worship** him. Many more believe he was a great teacher.

Just some of the things which might remind us of Jesus.

A scene from the Passion Play at Oberammergau in Germany. Each performance lasts for eight hours and involves 700 actors.

His story, together with his teachings, was written down in four books. Later they were included in the Bible, which has been translated into over a thousand languages.

Many people try to live their lives in the way they think Jesus would have wished. Some men and women spend their lives helping the poor and sick. Others give up money or power to do something special for him. There are even those who have been prepared to die because they believed in him.

We asked some thirteen-year-olds if they thought Jesus was important and why. Here are some of their answers.

JESUS WAS A PREACHER AND A GOOD MAN.

I THINK JESUS WAS QUITE TALL AND HAD A BEARD. I DON'T REALLY BELIEVE IN HIM.

JESUS WAS A MAN WHO CAME TO THIS PLANET TO SEE HOW PEOPLE WERE GETTING ON.

I BELIEVE IN JESUS. I BELIEVE HE CAME BACK FROM THE DEAD.

Mother Teresa is a **nun** who used to teach at a **convent** in Calcutta. The people outside the convent walls lived in great poverty. So she decided to leave the convent and help these people. She describes her reasons:

▶ We chose to be poor for love of God. In the service of the poorest of the poor. We are feeding the hungry Christ, clothing the naked Christ, taking care of the sick Christ and giving shelter to the homeless Christ.

Mother Teresa

Mother Teresa's work takes her all over the world.

▶ I was hungry and you fed me, thirsty and you gave me a drink; I was a stranger and you received me in your homes, naked and you clothed me; I was sick and you took care of me, in prison and you visited me.

The righteous will then answer him, 'When, Lord, did we ever see you hungry and feed you, or thirsty and give you a drink? . . .

The King will reply, 'I tell you, whenever you did this for one of the least important of these brothers of mine, you did it for me!'

Matthew 25:35–37,40

You do not have to look very far to find things which show that people believe Jesus is important: there may be churches close to your school; probably you have seen a priest or minister in your local town; and there are organisations, such as the Salvation Army and the Samaritans, who try to help people in need.

So it may seem odd that many people do not believe in Jesus at all. Some do not even believe that he existed; they think the story of his life is untrue. Others think that he *was* a real person – but they cannot accept that he was what he claimed to be.

Of course, if he did exist, we ought to be able to find some evidence to prove it. Even though it was so long ago, there may be some evidence that everyone would accept.

The early chapters of this book take you through some of that evidence. Then, you will be able to decide for yourself.

---

1 Write down each of these sentences. Beside each, write TRUE, FALSE or DON'T KNOW. For each one, explain how you decided.
   a) Jesus was a good man.
   b) Jesus never existed.
   c) Jesus was a great teacher.
   d) Jesus is important for some people.
   e) Jesus is still important for everyone.
2 Look at the drawing of the children on page 4. Choose any three statements. Write down whether you agree with them and give reasons.
3 a) Name four things which show us that people today still believe Jesus is important.
   b) Explain how each of them shows that Jesus is important.
4 a) Read the two passages on the left. Name four groups of people that Mother Teresa helps.
   b) Why do you think she decided to work among very poor people?
   c) Suggest two other ways in which a Christian could follow the teaching in Matthew's Gospel.
5 a) In groups, discuss the advantages of learning about the life of Jesus.
   b) Can you think of any disadvantages?

2 *What did Jesus Look Like?*

Think of any famous person in the world today. It can be a pop singer, sports player or anyone at all. Whoever you think of, you will know what he or she looks like. Today, we often see well-known people on television or in books.

Jesus has been a famous person for nearly 2000 years but you could not say what he looked like. No one can say what he looked like. Why not?

Pictures or statues cost money. Early Christians could not have afforded them. In any case, for many years after Jesus died, Christians were **persecuted**. It would not have been safe to have pictures of Jesus in your home.

But one early painting survived – just. The picture below shows a copy of it, made in 1847. The original was painted on a ceiling in the **catacombs** of Rome. The early Christians were buried there.

A copy of the first known picture of Jesus, painted sometime before CE 150.

It was painted by CE 150, perhaps a hundred years after Jesus died. So it is very unlikely that the painter ever met Jesus himself. Anyway, we can no longer be sure that this painting is an accurate copy because the original picture has decayed so badly.

However, you might wonder why we do not just read the Bible to find out what Jesus looked like. The reason is simple. The Bible does not tell us.

Jewish teachers wore beards, so Jesus probably did as well.

He would have had dark skin.

He must have been fit. He travelled so much on foot.

This picture is based on what we know about Jesus' life and people at the time.

We should not be surprised about that. The Bible began as stories passed on by word of mouth. Many of the listeners would have seen Jesus. They knew what he was like. Others knew he was a carpenter's son, an ordinary person just like themselves. So they would guess that he looked like them.

Perhaps the Bible says nothing because he was ugly.

I reckon they'd just forgotten.

I think he was about six foot tall with blue eyes and blond hair.

What do you think Jesus looked like?

There have been many films about Jesus. These are three actors who took the part of Jesus.

When people came to write down these stories, maybe they had forgotten what Jesus looked like. Or perhaps they did not think it was important. After all, it was what Jesus said and did that mattered.

But there is a more important question to ask about Jesus. How do we know he existed at all? Russian children, for instance, are taught that Jesus was invented in the second century CE.

What we need is *evidence*. But there are no pictures of Jesus painted in his lifetime and, of course, there were no cameras in those days. If we wanted to find out about a famous Roman, such as Julius Caesar, we could look at statues which were made of him.

But finding out about Jesus is not so easy. He was a poor Jew. He lived in a part of the Roman Empire which was not all that important. He was a preacher – but he was not the only one. And he was executed as a criminal – but so were many others. How will we find out about Jesus?

---

1 Copy out and complete this paragraph: The earliest known picture of _____ was found in the catacombs of _____ . This was where the early Christians were _____ . It was painted by CE _____ but the artist almost certainly did not meet Jesus.

2 a) Which picture on this page is most like your idea of Jesus? Explain why.
   b) Do you think it would be useful to know how Jesus looked? Give reasons for your view.

3 a) Write a description of what a friend in your class looks like. Include at least five details.

   b) Write a description of another person in your class. This time, do not write what they look like. Write about what kind of person they are.
   c) Some of you can read out your descriptions. See if you can guess whom you are talking about.
   d) Which is more important: (i) what people look like or (ii) what they are like as a person? Give reasons.

4 a) List all the kinds of evidence we might find about someone from 2000 years ago.
   b) Which kinds of evidence do you think we will find about Jesus? Explain how you decided.

3 *What the Jews and Romans Wrote*

When historians want to find out about the past, they use **primary sources**. These include writings from the actual time of the events they describe. So, if people wrote about Jesus nearly 2000 years ago, we can be reasonably sure that he did exist.

However, historians must also check these primary sources. Writers sometimes make mistakes; sometimes, they are **biased**. Often, we find out that they were not actually eye-witnesses after all; they relied on what someone else told them. And once in a while, a book turns out to be a complete fake.

Remember these points as you read the following two pages. They contain some of the most important early writings about Jesus.

Cornelius Tacitus (about CE 55–117)

Tacitus was a Roman who wrote a number of history books. He is thought to be one of the most reliable Roman historians. One of his books covers the years CE 14 to 68. In it, he describes a great fire in Rome in CE 64. Some people blamed this fire on the Emperor Nero; to stop this rumour, Nero blamed the Christians instead.

▶ Nero punished the Christians (as they were popularly called). Christ (from whom their name comes) had been executed by the governor of Judea, Pontius Pilate.

Roman Christians were executed by being sent to face hungry lions.

Tranquillus Suetonius (about CE 69–140?)

This Roman historian was the Emperor Hadrian's private secretary. So he probably used all sorts of official papers when writing his books. In about CE 112, he wrote a book about the Emperor Claudius, who reigned from CE 41 to 54. Here, he describes one of Claudius' actions:

▶ Christus urged on the Jews, who kept causing a disturbance. So Claudius sent them away from Rome.

The Talmud

This is a Jewish holy book, which was written early in the second century after Jesus died. However, people had passed its contents down by word of mouth from long before that.

▶ On the eve of Passover (a festival), they hanged Yeshu. He practised [black magic] and led Israel astray.

We know that Pontius Pilate was governor at about the time of Jesus' crucifixion.

Flavius Josephus (about CE 37–100?)

This Jewish historian was a priest's son. In CE 66 he led a Jewish revolt against the Romans in Galilee, but was captured. He went to live in Rome in CE 70, and became a Roman citizen. There, he wrote two books about the Jewish people. These are our best sources for Jewish history in the 1st century CE. At least some parts of these books are very accurate. This is what he wrote in CE 93–4:

▶ At about this time, Jesus was alive. He was a wise man, if you should call him a man. He achieved surprising feats and was a teacher. He got the support of many Jews and Greeks. He was the **Messiah.**

When Pilate had him condemned on the cross, those who had loved him from the start stood by him. On the third day they saw him alive again, as the holy **prophets** had predicted. And the Christians, named after him, are still with us today.

(Note: Josephus was not a Christian but his writing is biased in favour of Jesus. Later Christians may have added things to this passage. But it is almost certain that Josephus did write about Jesus.)

1 Write these sentences into your book. Beside each, write TRUE or FALSE. For each wrong one, write down what is wrong with it.
   a) Josephus led the Jews against the Romans.
   b) The Talmud is a book of magic.
   c) Tacitus wrote about the Emperor Claudius who said Christians started a fire in Rome.
   d) Suetonius probably used official records to help him write his books.
2 a) Jesus may have died in about CE 30. Which of the writers on these pages might have met him?
   b) Where do you think they got their facts from?
3 Read the extract from Josephus. Which parts of this might have been added by a Christian? Explain how you decided.
4 a) Divide your page into two columns, using a pencil and ruler. On the left, write EVIDENCE FOR JESUS' EXISTENCE. On the right, put DOUBTS ABOUT THE EVIDENCE.
   b) On the left, write down anything about Jesus given in these sources.
   c) On the right, list any reasons for having doubts about the evidence.

4 *What the Christians Wrote*

Early Christians met in their own homes or in the open air to hear about Jesus. The background scene shows the Sea of Galilee.

In the years after Jesus' death, his **apostles** and **disciples** told other people about the things he had said and done. They had probably learnt them by heart. That way, the same stories could be told over and over again.

At first, they did not need to write anything down. After all, the disciples had actually known Jesus. They knew what had happened. Anyway, Jesus had promised his disciples that he would return. If he came back soon, what was the point of writing it all down?

However, Christianity spread quickly over the next few years. **Missionaries**, such as Paul, travelled far and wide to tell people about Jesus and his message. New churches were set up and the Christian leaders had to keep in touch with them. So – at least from CE 50 – they wrote letters to them.

HOW WE MAY PROVE THAT THE BIBLE IS ACCURATE.

Picture 1: Archaeologists are always looking for early evidence of the Bible and they may even find earlier writing than this. It is possible that early Biblical writings may be found hidden away somewhere.

Picture 2: The early writings would prove whether copies made at a later time in history were accurate or not.

Picture 3: Archaeologists have also found evidence that events in the Bible really did happen. This does not prove that *all* of the Bible is true, but it means that the writers did not just make it all up.

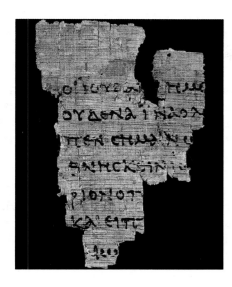

This piece of **papyrus** is part of John's Gospel. It is our oldest copy of the gospels, written within a century of Jesus' death.

The churches treasured these letters. Sometimes other churches borrowed them and made copies. Soon, a collection of them grew up. We can still read some of them today in the **New Testament**.

Some of Jesus' disciples may later have been put to death. As the rest grew old, their stories had to be written down, so that they would not be forgotten.

No one knows how many versions there were: many must have been lost. But four accounts survived to become part of the New Testament. Probably early Christians thought that they were the most accurate.

These books do not tell the story of the whole of Jesus' life. They were not written to do that. Their aim was to record what he taught – and to persuade people that he really was someone special – the Son of God.

In Britain, Christians called these writings by an Anglo-Saxon name, 'God-spel', which means 'good news'. Today, we call them 'gospels'.

The four gospels do not include their authors' names. But early Christians thought they were written by Matthew, Mark, Luke and John. Those are the names used in this book. One gospel which is not included in the Bible was written by someone called Thomas. It is a collection of stories about the childhood of Jesus. This is one of them.

▶ Jesus went through the village, and a lad ran and knocked against his shoulder. Jesus said to him: 'You shall not go further on your way', and the child immediately fell down and died.

The parents of the dead child came to Joseph and blamed him and said: 'Since you have such a child, you cannot dwell with us in the village; or else teach him to bless and not to curse. For he is slaying our children'.

And Joseph called the child aside and said: 'Why do you do such things that these people must suffer and hate us?' But Jesus replied: 'I know that these words are not yours; nevertheless for your sake I will be silent. But they shall bear their punishment.' And immediately those who had accused him became blind.

Infancy Gospel of St Thomas

1 Match up the words on the left with the correct description from the right.

disciple	person who travels to persuade people to join a religion
New Testament	a follower of Jesus
missionary	a record of Jesus' teaching and some of his life
gospel	the second part of the Christian Bible

2 Here is a list of reasons why people did not write about Jesus soon after he died. Write down those you think are correct.
a) Nobody had ever seen Jesus.
b) They thought no one would be interested.
c) The disciples could tell people about Jesus because they had met him.
d) They had nothing to write on.
e) People believed Jesus would return to earth.
3 Read Thomas' story about the young Jesus. Why do you think early Christians did not include these stories in the Bible?
4 a) Draw the scene beside Lake Galilee.
b) You are one of the people listening to the disciple beside the lake. Write down five questions you want to ask him about Jesus.

5   The Gospels

The Bible contains four gospels. Sometimes, their versions are very similar; some things turn up in all of them. At other times, they have different details; sometimes, they even disagree. How could this happen?

One obvious reason is that they were not written until years after Jesus died. In the meantime, people told the stories to their friends, and they told their friends, and so on. Think of how stories get passed round your school. Details can easily get changed.

Also, each writer included those details which were important *in his view*. Naturally, they had different ideas about this. Our modern newspapers often pick out different stories to put on their front pages. Each editor chooses what he or she thinks is most important or interesting.

Thirdly, each gospel was written for different people to read. This was bound to mean that their versions would be different. On the next page you can read what Adrian Mole wrote about school in his diary on 5 June.

The area around the Mediterranean Sea, showing where the four gospels were probably written and for whom they were written.

John's Gospel was written in about CE 95, probably for Christians living in Ephesus. The writer may have known Jesus' disciple called John. It is very different to the other Gospels and contains many different details. John sees Jesus as the Son of God; he is more concerned with what Jesus said than with his life.

Matthew's Gospel was written about CE 85 for Christians living at Antioch. People think the writer was Jewish. Matthew stresses Jesus' work as a teacher; but he also sees him as the son of God and the Messiah. He often refers to the Old Testament to show that prophets had foretold Jesus' arrival.

† Rome

BLACK SEA

● Athens

† Ephesus

† Antioch

CRETE

MEDITERRANEAN SEA

Caesarea †
●
Jerusalem ●
Bethlehem ●

PALESTINE

Mark's Gospel seems to be the earliest of the Synoptic Gospels, perhaps written by about CE 65. People think he may have got information direct from one of Jesus' disciples called Simon Peter. Its readers were Christians living in Rome. Mark shows Jesus as a very human person. He gets angry and he gets hurt just as other people do. Jesus calls himself the Son of Man, while others call him the Son of God.

Luke's Gospel dates from about CE 80. The writer was a Gentile (someone who was not Jewish); he wrote for other Gentiles living in Caesarea. He shows Jesus as a friend of all people, Jewish and Gentile; man, woman and child. Luke sees Jesus as the Messiah who has come to save everyone, not just the Jews.

Was used by

was used by

Was used by

Was used by

Mark — CE 65

Luke — CE 75–80

Q — CE?

Matthew — CE 85-90

▶ Miss Sproxton spotted my red socks in assembly! The old bag reported me to pop-eyed Scruton (the Headmaster). He had me in his office and gave me a lecture on the dangers of being a **nonconformist.** Then he sent me home to change into black socks.

Sue Townsend: *The Secret Diary of Adrian Mole.*

Suppose Adrian Mole had written an English essay about that day. Do you think he would have described events like that?

When we write something for someone else, we think of who they are; we think of what they are interested in. The gospel writers were the same. Each gospel was written to be read by different groups of Christians.

Mark's Gospel, for instance, was written for Christians living in Rome. It includes a number of Latin phrases which would only be understood by people who spoke the language. Also, Mark explains various Jewish customs. This would not have been needed if the readers had been Jews.

But, in many ways, Mark's Gospel is very similar to those of Matthew and Luke. They have a lot of the same stories; they look at Jesus' life in much the same way. So people call them the 'Synoptic Gospels'. It means they can be 'seen together' as giving one view of Jesus.

At times, these gospels use exactly the same words and phrases. Modern experts believe that Luke and Matthew copied from Mark. But this is not all: if you take Mark's account out of Matthew and Luke, there's still a lot left.

Much of what remains is too similar to be pure chance. Experts believe there was a lost book which Luke and Matthew used. They call it 'Q', as in the diagram above.

1 a) In groups, compare the front page news story in a number of newspapers *from the same day*.
   b) Write down the different headlines. Now, suggest reasons why the stories and headlines are different.
   c) Compare your results and views with those of other groups.
2 Divide a page of your book into four sections. Write the name of one gospel at the top of each section. Underneath, write these titles: WHEN IT MAY HAVE BEEN WRITTEN; WHERE IT WAS PROBABLY WRITTEN; WHO WOULD READ IT; HOW JESUS APPEARS. Then, fill in the information, using the words and map on page 12.
3 a) Read the following Bible passages: Mark 2:1–12; Luke 5:17–26; Matthew 9:1–8. How are these versions similar?
   b) Now read these passages: Mark 1:29–45; Matthew 8:1–4 and 8:14–17. What is the main difference between these?
   c) Suggest at least one reason why the versions are different.

6 What do you Know About Jesus?

As we have seen, the Bible tells us very little about what Jesus looked like. The writers were more interested in what he had to say. Yet most of us have our own idea of what he was like. And nearly everyone knows something about him.

We asked a group of twelve-year-olds to tell us what they knew about Jesus. The picture above shows what some of them told us.

Jesus lived nearly 2000 years ago. Obviously, these children never met him. Nor could they have talked to anyone who had. So where did they learn these things about him?

We asked them that, too. Below are some of their answers.

We then asked them which sources they thought were most reliable. Needless to say, they disagreed! The most reliable source was given the number one and the least reliable source was given the number seven.

One girl gave this order:

1 = Priest or minister
1 = Bible
3 Sunday School
4 = Teachers
4 = Parents
6 Television
7 Cinema

But one boy put this:

1 = Teachers
1 = Television
3 Sunday School
4 Bible
5 Priest or minister
6 Parents
7 Cinema

Finally, we added all the numbers together. The pupils used their calculators to check the adding up! Our final results are shown opposite.

The pupils had to give a reason for their top choice. One boy, who put his parents top, said, 'Parents are reliable because they're old.' Another boy said, 'The Bible is most reliable because it was written fairly near the time of Jesus so it will be pretty accurate'.

Christians have different views about the Bible. But most agree that the Bible gives them all they need to know about God. It shows them how they should live as followers of Jesus.

▶ The Catholic Church teaches that the whole Bible is the word of God. We say that it is inspired. We mean that God helped the writers in a special way. We have, therefore, a guarantee that the Bible is true.

But these writers wrote in the same way as anyone else would have written in those days. Each writer wrote in the way that suited him. Some of them were poets and so wrote poetry. All were trying to get across the truth of God.

Catholic Enquiry Centre: *God Speaks to us*

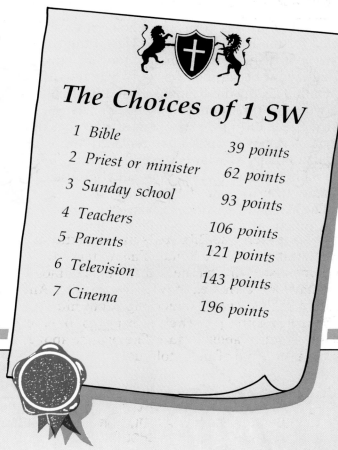

The Choices of 1 SW

1 Bible — 39 points
2 Priest or minister — 62 points
3 Sunday school — 93 points
4 Teachers — 106 points
5 Parents — 121 points
6 Television — 143 points
7 Cinema — 196 points

1 Write down at least two things you know about Jesus. Beside each fact, write down where you got your information from.
2 a) As a group, compare your answers. Each group could write them all out on a large sheet of paper.
   b) How many wrong 'facts' are there, as far as you can tell?
3 a) How much of your information is about Jesus as a young boy?
   b) Why do you think that is?
4 Now it's your turn!
   a) Put these seven sources in order of reliability (the most reliable comes top): Sunday School; cinema; priest or minister; teacher; Bible; television; parents.

   b) As a class, add up your marks and work out the final order.
   c) Discuss your results and see how they compare with our results above.
5 a) Write down the reasons for your top two choices.
   b) How do you think your parents or teachers found out about Jesus?
   c) Read the quotation above. Why do Catholics believe that the Bible is true?

7 *The World of Jesus*

Jesus lived in a country called Palestine, on the eastern edge of the Mediterranean Sea. More important, it was also on the very edge of the Roman Empire. The Romans had invaded the country in 63 BCE; they remained there throughout Jesus' life.

When Jesus was born, the whole area was ruled for the Romans by King Herod the Great. The Jews disliked the Romans; they also disliked King Herod because he was only half Jewish.

On his death, the Romans shared his kingdom between his three sons. His son, Archelaus, ruled Judea but made such a mess of it that the Romans removed him. They replaced him with a Roman official. Towards the end of Jesus' life, the man who had this job was called Pontius Pilate.

The arrival of a Roman governor did not help very much. Most of the people still hated being controlled by Romans. Even more, they hated having to pay taxes to them. These taxes helped pay for Roman soldiers to control the Jews.

Despite this, some Jews thought it was best to co-operate with the Romans. A number of the rich **Sadducees** were members of the Jewish Council, called the Sanhedrin. The Romans let this group make decisions about many local affairs in Judea.

But most Jews hoped that the Romans would either leave or be forced out of their country. Many people believed that the **scriptures** promised that God would send someone to free them. They called him the Messiah.

They even argued about what kind of person he would be. Some expected a warrior to fight the Romans; others said he would be a priest or a king – perhaps both. In a way, it did not matter which would happen. It gave the Jews hope for the future. That was what was important.

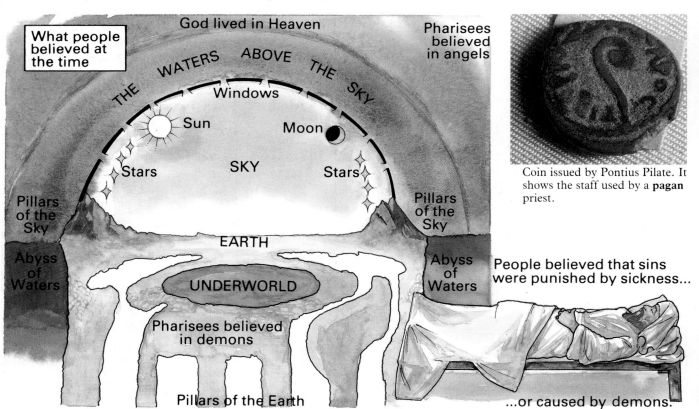

What people believed at the time

God lived in Heaven

THE WATERS ABOVE THE SKY

Windows

Sun

Moon

Stars   SKY   Stars

Pillars of the Sky

Pillars of the Sky

Abyss of Waters

Abyss of Waters

EARTH

UNDERWORLD

Pharisees believed in demons

Pillars of the Earth

Pharisees believed in angels

Coin issued by Pontius Pilate. It shows the staff used by a **pagan** priest.

People believed that sins were punished by sickness...

...or caused by demons.

▶ Some **Pharisees** and some members of Herod's party were sent to Jesus to trap him with questions. They came to him and said, 'Teacher, we know that you tell the truth, without worrying about what people think . . . Tell us, is it against our Law to pay taxes to the Roman Emperor? Should we pay them or not?'

But Jesus saw through their trick and answered, 'Why are you trying to trap me? Bring a silver coin, and let me see it.'

They brought him one, and he asked, 'Whose face and name are these?'

'The Emperor's,' they answered.

So Jesus said, 'Well, then, pay the Emperor what belongs to the Emperor, and pay God what belongs to God.'

And they were amazed at Jesus.

Mark 12:13–17

On another Sabbath Jesus went into a **synagogue** and taught. A man was there whose right hand was **paralysed**. Some teachers of the Law and some Pharisees wanted a reason to accuse Jesus of doing wrong, so they watched him closely to see if he would heal on the Sabbath.

But Jesus knew their thoughts and said to the man, 'Stand up and come here to the front.' The man got up and stood there.

Then Jesus said to them, 'I ask you: What does our Law allow us to do on the Sabbath? To help or to harm? To save a man's life or destroy it?' He looked around at them all; then he said to the man, 'Stretch out your hand.' He did so, and his hand became well again.

They were filled with rage and began to discuss among themselves what they could do to Jesus.

Luke 6:1–2; 6–11

Sadducees:
A small but important group of Jews who supported the Romans. They believed totally in the law God gave to Moses (the first five books of the Old Testament).

Sadducees

Zealots:
A small extreme group who believed in fighting to get rid of the Romans. They

Zealots

Pharisees:
A larger but respected group of Jews. They believed the Messiah would come. They had added to the Law of Moses. They would have nothing to do with Gentiles or sinners.

Pharisees

were active from the time of Herod's death to CE70.

Three Jewish groups and their ideas.

▶ Jesus was walking through some cornfields on the **Sabbath.** His disciples began to pick the ears of corn, rub them in their hands, and eat the grain. Some Pharisees asked, 'Why are you doing what our Law says you cannot do on the Sabbath?'...

1 Copy out and complete this paragraph:
Jesus grew up in _____ which was part of the _____ Empire. When Jesus was born, it was ruled by King _____ the _____ . Later, the Romans used their own officials to govern Judea. At the end of Jesus' life, this man was _____ _____ .

2 a) Draw the map on page 26.
b) Write a few sentences to explain who these people were: Sadducees; Pharisees; Zealots.
c) Which of these groups do you think would have been most annoyed by the coin on page 16? Give a reason for your answer.
d) Imagine that your country was occupied by an enemy. Which of the following words would describe your feelings? (You may add others, if you wish.) Give reasons for each choice. Miserable; happy; sad; angry; delighted; bitter; wanting revenge; not interested; wanting to fight back; relieved; proud?

3 a) Read the passage from Mark's Gospel (12:13–17). What might have happened to Jesus if he had said they should not pay the taxes?
b) What do you think a Zealot would have thought of Jesus' answer?
c) Why was it a clever answer?

These children are taking part in a play. It tells the world's most famous story. Every Christmas, it is acted out when Christians remember the birth of Jesus. It is always much the same. A baby boy is born in a stable and three men bring him gifts.

But was it really like that? Is the story that you know the same as the one in early Christian writings? More important, most of the gospel content is about Jesus' teaching. So why does the Bible include the story at all?

Only two of the gospels, Matthew and Luke, describe Jesus' birth. Experts claim that one tells it from Joseph's point of view; the other tells it from Mary's. This is part of Matthew's version.

▶ Jesus was born in the town of Bethlehem in Judea, during the time when Herod was king. Soon afterwards, some men who studied the stars came from the east to Jerusalem and asked, 'Where is the baby born to be the king of the Jews? We saw his star when it came up in the east, and we have come to worship him.'

When King Herod heard about this, he was very upset, and so was everyone else in Jerusalem. He called together all the chief priests and the teachers of the Law and asked them, 'Where will the Messiah be born?'

'In the town of Bethlehem in Judea,' they answered. 'For this is what the prophet wrote' . . .

And so they left, and on their way they saw the same star they had seen in the east. When they saw it, how happy they were, what joy was theirs! It went ahead of them until it stopped over the place where the child was.

They went into the house, and when they saw the child with his mother Mary, they knelt down and worshipped him. They brought out their gifts of gold, frankincense and myrrh, and presented them to him.

Matthew 2:1–5; 9–11

The wise men visit Jesus. From a Korean Nativity play.

No crib for a bed . . .

By the time Matthew was writing, Jesus' teaching had become well-known. But, when he was born, few people were there to watch the event. He was not born anywhere special and there were no crowds waiting for the news.

Instead, Matthew tells us a story of wise men from the east. They would have been Gentiles, yet they had travelled far to see the baby. They had even brought special gifts. For them, Jesus' birth was important.

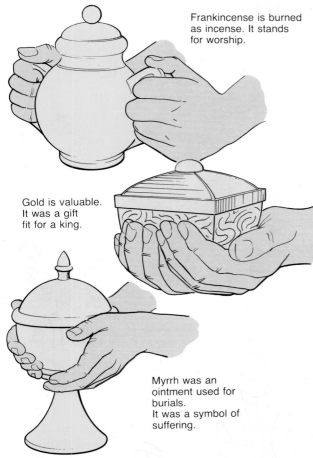

Frankincense is burned as incense. It stands for worship.

Gold is valuable. It was a gift fit for a king.

Myrrh was an ointment used for burials. It was a symbol of suffering.

The wise men brought gifts – but they were not ordinary presents. Each one had a meaning, according to Matthew's Gospel.

Some events in the story, such as the star which guided these men, are mentioned in the Old Testament. Christians think of them as symbols which show how important Jesus' birth was. They are signs that this was no ordinary birth. This baby was the Messiah. The one the prophets had said God would send one day.

So the birth stories remind Christians that Jesus was not just special in later life, when he started teaching. He was also special from the moment that his mother became pregnant.

Jesus' birth was a great event. There are stories like it about many great religious leaders. After Jesus' death, Christians wanted to hear about his birth. The story is important because of its *meaning* to Christians, not just because of the details themselves.

Birth Certificate

Name ————————
Date of birth ————————
Place of birth ————————
Name of mother ————————
Name of father ————————
Home town of parents ————————
————————
Witnesses ————————
————————

This imaginary birth certificate is for use with question 1. (People *did* have to **notify** births at this time.)

Luke tells the birth story in chapter 2:1–20. Read this and Matthew 1:18–25 before answering these questions.

1 Copy out the birth certificate above and fill in as many details as you can.
2 Explain in your own words why Jesus' birth is important to Christians.
3 How do the two gospels differ about:
   a) Where Mary and Joseph lived?
   b) The news that Mary was to give birth to Jesus?
   c) Which gospel do you think tells the story from Mary's viewpoint? Give reasons for your choice.
4 a) Read page 18. How many men are mentioned bringing gifts?
   b) Why do you think pictures usually show three of them?
   c) Each of their gifts was a symbol. What do they tell Christians about Jesus' life?
   d) Choose one other symbolic gift to give Jesus. Explain your choice.
5 Suppose you were one of these people: a shepherd; one of the men bringing gifts; a guest at the inn. Write your own account of going to see the baby Jesus.

The Little Lord Jesus . . .

The gospels are written *by* Christians *for* Christians. They are passing on the 'good news' about Christ. They do not claim to be history books, although Luke was careful with details of history.

However, we have seen evidence that Jesus was alive in the first century CE, so he must have been born. But was he really born in the way the gospels describe? The honest answer is, 'We don't know'.

Many of our Christmas customs only came to Britain quite recently. This picture shows some of them. It includes (on the right) a Christingle.

But we can be fairly sure about one thing. Jesus was almost certainly *not* born on 25 December. According to the gospels, shepherds were in the fields, keeping watch over their sheep when Jesus was born. But they generally stopped doing this during October, because it became too cold and wet. So experts think that Jesus was probably born in the early Autumn.

The date of 25 December was chosen by Bishop Julius, but not until the fourth century CE. It was a good time to choose because it was already a great Roman festival, called Saturnalia.

Pagans across Europe worshipped the sun god at this time and they enjoyed feasts. The Christians took over the festival and kept the feasts. The pagans had lit bonfires for their sun god; Christians worshipped the Son of God instead.

Some Christian customs have disappeared. One of the most unusual ones took place in the Scottish Hebrides islands until early this century. It was based on a verse from Matthew's Gospel.

Jesus had arrived at Capernaum and wanted to teach in the temple. But first there was a tax to pay. He told Simon Peter:

▶ . . . go to the lake and drop in a line. Pull up the first fish you hook, and in its mouth you will find a coin worth enough for my temple-tax and yours. Take it and pay them our taxes.

Matthew 17:27

There was a tradition in the Western Isles off Scotland that Jesus had told Peter to row exactly 707 strokes before dropping the line for the fish with the coin. So, each Christmas Day, the young fishermen got into their boats and rowed 707 strokes. All the fish they caught were given to the poor as a Christmas gift. They called it the Hebrides Tribute.

Lay down his Sweet Head

In which year was Jesus born?
The Bible does not give a date for Jesus' birth, but it includes these details:

▶ During the time when Herod was king of Judea . . .
At that time the Emperor Augustus ordered a **census** to be taken throughout the Roman Empire. When this first census took place, Quirinius was the governor of Syria.

Luke 1:5; 2:1–2

But these details cannot *all* be right. The first census *did* take place when Quirinius was governor – but this did not happen when King Herod was on the throne. King Herod died in 4 BCE.

People have come up with various ways of solving this problem. Of course, Luke could just have got it wrong. However, he was usually careful with his facts. One answer may be that Quirinius finished the census, although it began years earlier. This would fit with Jesus being born in about 5 or 4 BCE.

But how could Jesus have been born in 5 BCE? This may sound impossible – but it's one of the easiest questions to answer! The dating system of BC and AD was first worked out in CE 525 by a monk.

He counted backwards to Jesus' birth and a new system of dates was created. On his system, the year 1 AD (CE) was the year of Jesus' birth, but he got his sums slightly wrong.

The Hebrides Tribute was featured on this British postage stamp.

The prisoner in a stable
Geoffrey Bull was a missionary who was made a prisoner by the Chinese in 1951. They held him for three years. Here, he describes his first Christmas as a prisoner:

▶ It was Christmas Eve and here I was in an eastern stable. It was a wretched place. The smell of the animals filled the air; straw and dung lay underfoot.

My thoughts travelled back to that first Christmas Eve and that little stable at Bethlehem where Jesus was born. It was a place like this, I thought.

I forgot all about being a prisoner. I felt so thankful and full of worship. I had no gold, no myrrh, no frankincense to bring. But all at once that stable was a holy place. Jesus himself was there.

I gave the hay to the horse and lay down on the boards. I felt very near to my Lord that night, for Jesus, we are told, had nowhere either to lay his head.

G T Bull: Prisoner Beyond the River

---

1 a) Draw the Christingle shown opposite. Each part is a symbol of something else. Which part do you think represents: (i) Jesus' blood; (ii) the fruits of the earth; (iii) the world; (iv) Jesus as 'the Light of the World'?
   b) What do you think 'Light of the World' means?
2 Write down things which Christians are reminded of at Christmas. What other things does it remind you of?
3 a) Read the story of the Hebrides Tribute. In groups, think of what we could do today to celebrate Christmas.
   b) Compare the groups' answers. Discuss which one is most suitable.
4 a) Look at these sentences from two Christmas cards: (i) *Wishing you a very happy Christmas;* (ii) *May peace and joy be yours this Christmas.* Which one do you think is most suitable for Christmas? Why?
   b) Design your own Christmas card as if it came from a Christian in India or Africa. Draw it *without* words or people. Afterwards, you could have a vote to decide which one best sums up the spirit of Christmas.

9 *Jesus Grows Up*

A painting called *Christ in the House of His Parents* by Millais.

Jesus grew up in Nazareth, which was only a small place in those days. In fact, the Old Testament does not even mention it. The New Testament tells us very little about Jesus' childhood there. However, we can still piece together the evidence.

This is what Mark's Gospel tells us about Jesus later in his life:

▶ Jesus . . . went back to his home town, followed by his disciples. On the Sabbath he began to teach in the synagogue. Many people were there; and when they heard him, they were all amazed.

'Where did he get all this?' they asked. 'What wisdom is this that has been given him? . . . Isn't he the carpenter, the son of Mary, and the brother of James, Joseph, Judas, and Simon? Aren't his sisters living here?' And so they rejected him.

Mark 6:1 – 3

MAIN FOODS: BREAD, WATER AND VEGETABLES...

ON HOLY DAYS AND SPECIAL OCCASIONS PEOPLE ATE MEAT AND DRANK RED WINE...

MEAT AND BREAD WERE BROKEN WITH THE FINGERS.

Food and drink in Jesus' time.

All Jewish boys had to learn to speak Hebrew; the Old Testament was written in that language. Jesus could read it, too. This suggests that Jesus had a good education, probably at the local synagogue.

As a young boy, Jesus would have gone to the synagogue in Nazareth with his parents. He would have spent the service with his mother in a separate part of the building, perhaps behind a wall or curtain. From about the age of thirteen, he would have joined the men.

A rabbi led these services; the word means 'teacher'. But members of the **congregation** could also help. Some led the **prayers**; others would read the scriptures and explain them. Any adult Jewish man could do this. So it was natural for Jesus to begin his teaching in the synagogues.

But Jesus would also have helped his father in his business. The Bible calls Joseph a 'carpenter' and he probably ran his business from home. In those days, carpenters were more like modern builders. Joseph would have been a skilled woodworker, but he would have done other building jobs too.

We know very little about Jesus' family – but we know even less about Joseph. The last time we hear of him was when Jesus was just twelve. They all went to Jerusalem for the Passover festival. Many people think Joseph must have died before Jesus began preaching.

The inside of a synagogue. (The one in Nazareth would have been smaller.)
Look for:
- the rabbi (the man leading the service);
- the menorah (candlestick with seven branches);
- the ark (the cupboard containing the Jewish Law); and
- the bimah (the raised platform, used for readings).

---

1 Match up the words on the left with the correct description from the right.

rabbi	cupboard containing the Torah
bimah	man who teaches the Jewish Law
ark	seven-branched candlestick
menorah	raised platform in the centre of a synagogue

2 a) Read the passage on page 22 from Mark's Gospel. What is wisdom?
b) Write down the names of two people whom you think are wise. Explain why you have chosen them.

c) Why didn't the people from Nazareth expect a carpenter's son to be wise?

3 a) Look at the drawing opposite. Why do you think meat was not eaten often?
b) How do you think they cooked their meals?
c) Write down at least five ways in which Jesus' life was different from yours.
d) Does this mean he was more or less happy than you are? Explain your answer.

4 a) Read Matthew 13:55. How does this differ from what Mark says on page 22?
b) If Jesus were a carpenter, what sort of person do you think this would have made him? (Think about the kind of work a carpenter must do.)

10 Lost in Jerusalem

Jews still pray at the Western Wall in Jerusalem.

Look at the picture above. It shows Jews praying beside a wall in Jerusalem. Jewish families who visit the city today make a point of going there.

The reason is that this is a very ancient and special wall indeed. It is all that remains of the Temple which was built here by King Herod after 20 BCE.

Like an earlier Temple, it did not last. In CE70, Roman armies captured Jerusalem and Herod's Temple was eventually destroyed. Many people believe that Jesus foretold this event (in Luke 21:20–21).

It was not actually finished until after Jesus' death. However, even in his lifetime, it was magnificent. Its holiest places had been built by a thousand priests, specially trained to do the job. It even had golden spikes on top to stop birds roosting! Each morning, silver trumpets announced sunrise.

When Jesus was twelve years old, he and his parents made the trip to Jerusalem. They went in a large party because there was safety in numbers. They had to pass through Samaria. The Samaritans and the Jews did not get on with each other.

But this was a very special trip. Jesus' family were not just going to Jerusalem. They would be there for the festival of Passover. It reminds the Jews of the time when they escaped from Egypt where they had been slaves, around 1250 BCE.

Jews throughout the Roman Empire would also be making the journey. The city would have been full of people. And nowhere would have been more crowded than the Temple.

It was not just because it was holy that the Temple was special to the Jews. The Romans controlled Jerusalem. But the Jews controlled the Temple. They could even insist that Roman coins were not used there.

More important, they could only offer **sacrifices** in the Temple, nowhere else. Often, they sacrificed animals or birds. But they could offer vegetables, too. This was a way of thanking God – or of asking for his forgiveness.

As it was Passover, Mary and Joseph probably sacrificed a lamb in the Temple. But, when they had set off for home, they found Jesus was missing. Back they went to Jerusalem, looking for him. They found him in the Temple.

▶ His parents were astonished when they saw him, and his mother said to him, 'My son, why have you done this to us? Your father and I have been terribly worried trying to find you.'

He answered them, 'Why did you have to look for me? Didn't you know that I had to be in my Father's house?' But they did not understand his answer.

Luke 2:48–50

A model of the Temple.

1 People went to the Outer Court first.
  (People who were not Jewish could not go any further.)

2 There were traders selling animals and birds to be sacrificed. Each person tried to get the best animal they could afford.

4 Next, people went into the Women's Court. This was as far as women and children were allowed to go.

5 The men finally went into the Court of Israel. From here, they could see:

6 The altar where the animals were sacrificed.

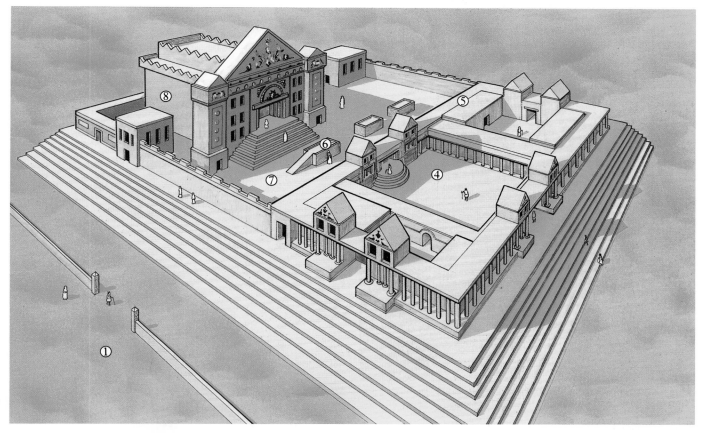

Plan of the Temple (see question 1).

3 There were also people changing money. Roman coins had a picture of the emperor's head on them and so were not allowed inside the Temple. So people swapped their Roman coins for special Temple coins.

7 Only priests were allowed into the Court of Priests.

8 The holiest part was called 'The Holy of Holies'. Only the High Priest ever went into it – just once a year, when he asked God to forgive the sins of all Jewish people.

1 a) Make an outline drawing of the Temple shown above.
  b) Mark on it each of the places mentioned in the captions.
  c) Why was the holiest part called 'The Holy of Holies'?

2 a) Give three reasons why the Temple was very special to Jews.
  b) Why do you think the Romans let the Jews keep control of the Temple?
  c) Why do you think Roman coins could not be used there?

3 a) What is a sacrifice?
  b) Why did the Jews make sacrifices in the Temple?
  c) Sacrifices were common in ancient times. Why do you think they are now rare in most countries?

4 a) Read the passage on page 24 from Luke's Gospel. Who was Jesus speaking of when he said 'my Father'?
  b) Why do you think his parents did not understand him?

║║ *A Voice in the Desert*

This picture comes from the film *Jesus of Nazareth*. It shows John baptising Jesus at Aenon.

Years passed and Jesus grew up. What happened to him in all that time we do not know. When the Bible next mentions him, he is a grown man.

Before that, someone else has appeared. This is Jesus' cousin. He is a travelling preacher called John. This news report has all the details.

'God's Kingdom Coming Soon' claims desert wild man

▶ God is about to send someone very important to the Jews. That is the message being spread by a man they call John 'the Baptist'.

People should ask God's forgiveness *now*, he claims. He advises those who are really sorry for what they have done wrong to be **baptised** in the River Jordan.

John himself is carrying out these baptisms. But he warns people that they must change their way of life. They must be honest and do things which please God.

Our local correspondent in Aenon writes, 'Many people are coming out to see this unusual man. Lots of

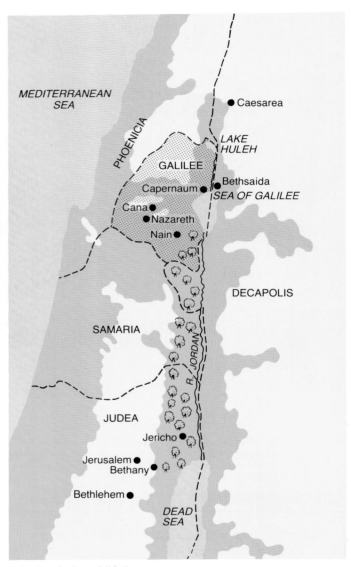

Palestine in Jesus' lifetime.

people are taking up his invitation to be baptised. They walk into the river and he dips them under the water. He claims that it's a sign that they've had their sins washed away.'

John is a strange-looking man. His hair is not cut, and he wears a beard. His only clothing is a tunic made of camel skin, with a leather belt round his waist.

He seems to eat very little. People think he must live on wild food, but there is very little out in the desert, mainly insects and honey.

Two modern baptisms. On the left: a baptism of a baby beside the font. Above: a baptism of an adult believer in a river.

Our religious expert comments, 'John is a priest's son. People say that he was a miracle baby. His mother was very old when he was born and his father thought he saw an angel.

'He did not believe the angel when it told him that his wife would have a baby. In fact, he was struck dumb for nine months. At least, that's what people are saying!'

Other reports say that people believe that John is a prophet, a messenger sent by God. Some even claim that he is the ancient prophet Elijah, born again.

Ordinary folk see all this as a sign that God will soon create his Kingdom of peace on earth.

However, experts do not believe he is the prophet Elijah, and John himself says he is not the Messiah. He even denies that he is a prophet. He sees himself simply as someone who has a message to give about the Messiah. From what he says, it seems that someone is coming to judge us for what we are doing.

John talks in pictures. He speaks of trees being chopped down if they don't produce fruit. He seems to think that the world as we know it is about to end.

1 Explain the meaning of
(i) forgiveness; (ii) baptism; (iii) prophet; (iv) Messiah.
2 a) Look at the two pictures on this page. Which one do you think is most like the baptisms given by John? Explain how you decided.
b) Why did John choose a place like Aenon?
3 a) What are the differences between the two baptism scenes? You should find at least three.
b) Why do you think the adults wish to be baptised?
4 a) Draw John the Baptist, using the information on page 26.
b) Work in pairs. Imagine you were the reporter who wrote this 'news story'. Write down four questions you would have asked John.
c) Pass these questions to your friend. Now, imagine you were John. Write down the answers you would have given.
d) As a group, compare your questions and answers.

12 A Turning-Point

John baptising Jesus. A fifth-century Italian **mosaic**.

Jesus was one of those who came to John to be baptised. We are not sure how old Jesus then was but Luke's Gospel gives us two clues. It says that:

- Jesus was about thirty years old.
- the word of God came to John during the fifteenth year of Emperor Tiberius' reign.

Historians believe that Tiberius became Emperor in CE 14. If that is correct, John began preaching in CE 28. So that is the earliest year in which Jesus could have been baptised.

We are not sure, either, where the baptism took place. John's Gospel mentions 'Bethany', which is on the far side of the River Jordan. This is where John was baptising at the time. Bethany seems to be the most probable place of Jesus' baptism.

John may have known Jesus; Luke says that Jesus' mother, Mary, was a cousin of John's mother, Elizabeth. Mary even visited Elizabeth after the Angel Gabriel had told Mary that she would give birth to Jesus.

Of course, the two families may not have been all that close. But there is a chance that Elizabeth had mentioned Jesus to John; she may have repeated what the angel had told Mary about him.

However, we can be fairly sure about one thing. The gospels agree that Jesus *was* baptised, although only Matthew and Mark say that John carried out the baptism.

▶ ... Jesus arrived from Galilee and came to John at the Jordan to be baptised by him. But John tried to make him change his mind. 'I ought to be baptized by you,' John said, 'and yet you have come to me!'

But Jesus answered him, 'Let it be so for now. For in this way we shall do all that God requires.' So John agreed.

As soon as Jesus was baptised, he came up out of the water. Then heaven was opened to him, and he saw the Spirit of God coming down like a dove and alighting on him. Then a voice said from heaven, 'This is my own dear Son, with whom I am pleased.'

Matthew 3:13–17

The dove was seen as a symbol of God's Spirit. Like God's Spirit the dove is pure and brings peace. As he came out of the water, Jesus was given the power to help him to do whatever God wished.

This was a turning-point in Jesus' life. As he set off into the desert, he was leaving behind his former life. Things would never be quite the same again.

Father Borrelli amongst the Scugnizzi.

Father Borrelli is a Roman Catholic priest who lives in Italy. He is very concerned about the homeless young people of Naples. People call them 'scugnizzi'.

He decided to help them. Here, he describes that decision – *his* turning-point.

▶ It was becoming increasingly clear to me that it was the scugnizzi whom I really wanted to help. Everything that one heard and saw of them was horrifying.

Gangs of homeless children roaming the streets of Naples all night meant nothing to [the authorities]. What could I do for them? And what could I possibly do alone?

(Shortly afterwards, he met an old college friend.)

'The scugnizzi, Ciccio.'

'Yes, a terrible problem – terrible.' He looked at me again. 'But Mario, what on earth could you hope to do?'

'There's only one thing for it,' I said. 'I shall become a scugnizzo myself.'

At that moment, the matter became quite definite. By saying it aloud, I had committed myself, and I would never draw back.

Father Borrelli: *A Street Lamp and the Stars*

The Son of God

Jesus is sometimes described in the Gospels as 'the Son of God'. What does it mean?

Early Christians believed that Jesus had a very special relationship with God. Some stories tell of the voice of God calling Jesus 'my Beloved Son'.

Jesus himself called God 'Abba'. It was a word used by a child to talk to his father. Yet Jews in those days did not use such a personal name when they prayed to God.

But 'Son of God' meant something else to Jews. They seem to have used it as another title for the Messiah. Much later in Jesus' life, he was asked, 'Are you the Christ (Messiah), the Son of God?'

1 Copy out and complete:
Jesus came from _____ to the River _____. John was _____ at Jesus' request for a baptism. As Jesus rose from the water, God's _____ _____ came down like a _____. A voice was heard from _____ saying, 'This is my own _____ _____ , with whom I am pleased.'

2 a) Look at the picture on page 28. Write down who or what you can see under the letters A, B, C and D.
b) How has the person tried to show God the Father?

3 a) From what you have read about Elizabeth and Mary, do you think John would already have known about Jesus? Give reasons.
b) Read the extract from Matthew's Gospel. Does it sound as if John knew of Jesus? Again, give reasons.
c) Explain in your own words what 'Son of God' means.

4 a) Read about Father Borrelli opposite. Why was this his 'turning-point'?
b) Write down an example of a turning-point in your life or that of someone you know. Explain in detail what happened and how life changed afterwards.

The Three Temptations of Christ, a painting by Botticelli.

Have you ever been in a situation where you did not know what to do? You had to make a choice. Perhaps you felt that you wanted to do one thing, but, deep inside, you knew it was wrong. This is what we call being tempted.

Jesus went through this after his baptism. The baptism seems to have been a very special experience for him – a special experience of God. After this event, Jesus had to think carefully about what had happened. After all, if he really was God's son, he had an important decision to make. What was he going to do about it?

So he went out into the desert, where the land was probably bare and dry. The gospel stories say he spent forty nights there. Some Christians believe the number 'forty' is a symbol. It is like talking about a long period of time without being exact about the real number of days.

The three temptations.

During that time he fasted, which means he ate nothing; at night, he probably slept in caves. However, the gospels are careful not to say he went without water. He would have died if he had had nothing to drink.

Once there, he found himself tempted. The gospels mention three separate temptations but Jesus was possibly tempted in other ways, too. One writer believed he was tempted the whole time he was in the desert.

But who tempted Jesus? Matthew says it was Satan – a Hebrew word which means 'tempter'. The other two gospels use a more well-known name: they write of the tempter as the Devil.

Did Jesus see a real person talking to him? Certainly, the Bible writers thought he did. Many people in Jesus' time thought the Devil was just as real as God himself. Some modern Christians would agree with this.

But there are other ways of understanding this figure. One way is to see Satan as another symbol. He stands for evil, for doing all those things which do not please God.

Perhaps what was happening was that Jesus was working through in his own mind what kind of Messiah he should be. Step by step, he thought about the different things he might do. And one by one, he rejected each idea.

This girl is facing temptation.

The next time we come across him, he has started preaching, telling people that God's Kingdom is coming. By then, he had made his decision.

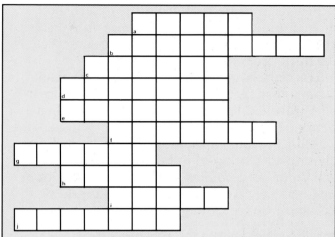

1 Copy out this crossword and fill in the answers, using the clues below.

   a) The number of temptations.
   b) Jesus made a number of these in the desert.
   c) Where Jesus was tempted to 'take a jump'.
   d) Original meaning of 'Satan'.
   e) Act of cleansing by water.
   f) One of the gospels containing the story.
   g) The place where Jesus went to think.
   h) Another name for Satan.
   i) The number of days in the desert.
   j) Going without food for some time.

Now, copy down the word which reads downwards and explain what it means.

2 Look at the Botticelli painting. Write a sentence explaining which temptation is shown by each of the letters.
3 Write down all the symbols you can find in the story and explain what each one stands for. (Clue: forty days and nights.)
4 a) In groups, find out what ideas each person has about the Devil. Then, share your findings with another group.
   b) Do you think Jesus had 'seen the Devil'? Give reasons for your answer.

14 *Disciples and Apostles*

When Jesus came back from the desert, he moved into Capernaum, a town on the western shore of the Sea of Galilee. This became the base for his journeys around the area.

His preaching attracted many people. Luke tells us that there were women, as well as men, who travelled round with him. Some of them became his 'disciples' – his pupils.

After praying all night on a mountain, Jesus chose twelve of them to be a special group. We call them his '**apostles**'. The word means 'sent out' and they were called this because they became Jesus' messengers.

▶ 'I have chosen you to be with me,' he told them. 'I will also send you out to preach, and you will have **authority** to drive out demons.'

Mark 3:14–15

In the army, a soldier is commissioned. This means he is given a special job to do. He must be **loyal** to the Queen and to his superior officers.

In the same way, Jesus commissioned the twelve disciples. They had to be loyal to him.

And their special job was to help him spread the good news of the Kingdom of God. Later, they became the leaders of the new Christian Church.

They were a strange group of men – not the sort of people you might have thought Jesus would pick to help him.

▶ As Jesus walked along the shore of Lake Galilee, he saw two fishermen, Simon and his brother Andrew, catching fish with a net. Jesus said to them, 'Come with me, and I will teach you to catch men.' At once, they left their nets and went with him.

He went a little farther on and saw two other brothers, James and John, the sons of Zebedee. They were in their boat getting their nets ready. As soon as Jesus saw them, he called them; they left their father Zebedee in their boat with the hired men and went with Jesus.

Mark 1:16–20

▶ As he walked along, he saw a tax collector, named Matthew, sitting in his office. He said to him, 'Follow me.' Matthew got up and followed him.

Matthew 9:9

This is a view of Capernaum by the Sea of Galilee. The remains of a synagogue from the 2nd Century CE are still there.

SIMON is a **Zealot** and a fighter in the **underground movement.** Ready to die for what he believes in. Very religious. He is sure God wants him to fight the Romans and drive them out of Palestine.

THOMAS will not believe things until he has seen the proof. He seems to think that 'seeing is believing'.

JAMES and JOHN (brothers). Also fishermen from Galilee, but seem to be comfortably off. Their father employs people to work for him; their mother is ambitious and wants them to do well. They get impatient with people who cross them. Friends have nicknamed them 'the sons of thunder'.

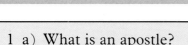

SIMON (also known as PETER). A fisherman from Galilee, he speaks with a strong local accent. He is boastful and speaks his mind. He acts before he thinks and can be violent if he is put into a corner. He has been known to lie to get himself out of trouble.

---

1 a) What is an apostle?
  b) Read the notes on the five apostles. For each one, give at least one reason why religious Jews might have thought he was unsuitable.
2 Read the passages from the Bible.
  a) What features are the same in both stories?
  b) Write down anything which surprises you about either story.
  c) What do these stories tell us about Jesus?
3 Read each of the descriptions below of the twelve apostles. Try to guess who is being described. Some of the clues are followed by references to passages in the Bible. These will help you to find out which apostle is being described. Write down the answers in your book.
  A The disciple who tried to walk on water (Matthew 14:29).
  B The disciple who took his brother to meet Jesus (John 1:40–41).
  C A disciple who helped prepare the Passover meal (Luke 22:8).
  D One of the brothers who left his father to follow Jesus (Matthew 4:21).
  E A tax collector.
  F A son of Alphaeus (Luke 6:15).
  G Jesus saw him under a fig tree. He was also called Bartholomew (John 1:48).
  H A Zealot.
  I Disciple who had to see Jesus before he believed he was alive (John 20:24–5).
  J He lived in Bethsaida (John 1:44).
  K Disciple who betrayed Jesus with a kiss (Matthew 26:14–15).
  L The twelfth disciple (Matthew 10:3).
4 Draw a 'wanted' poster asking for people to become apostles. You should include details about what sort of people are needed. For instance, should they be married or single?

15 Jesus and the Sinners

People called Jesus 'rabbi', which means 'teacher'. In those days, Jews expected a rabbi to behave in a certain way. They certainly did not expect him to have anything to do with **outcasts**.

There were also people known as 'sinners' who did not keep the Jewish Law. And it was thought wrong to enter the house of a Gentile (anyone who was not a Jew). To eat with any of these people was thought to make you unclean.

Of all the people whom the Jews disliked, **tax-collectors** probably came top of the list. The Romans did not collect taxes themselves; they sold the job to whoever paid most to do it.

Perhaps that sounds strange, but it worked like this. One man might say, 'If you give me the job, I'll collect £10 000 in this area.' Another man might say, 'I will collect £12 000'.

The bidding went on until no one could go any higher. The person with the highest bid got the job. He was then free to collect whatever he could from the people. This way, he made his living – and a fat profit! You can see why Jews did not like tax-collectors.

Think what they might feel about Jesus' actions in the following story.

Prejudice means judging someone without knowing enough about them. This fan has no good reason for his opinion – so he is *prejudiced*.

▶ Jesus went on into Jericho and was passing through. There was a chief tax collector there named Zacchaeus, who was rich. He was trying to see who Jesus was, but he was a little man and could not see Jesus because of the crowd.

So he ran ahead of the crowd and climbed a sycamore tree to see Jesus . . . When Jesus came to that place, he looked up and said to Zacchaeus, 'Hurry down, Zacchaeus, because I must stay in your house today.'

Zacchaeus hurried down and welcomed him with great joy. All the people who saw it started grumbling, 'This man had gone as a guest to the home of a sinner!'

Zacchaeus stood up and said to the Lord, 'Listen, sir! I will give half my belongings to the poor, and if I have cheated anyone, I will pay him back four times as much.'

Luke 19:1–8

The strict Jews were amazed that a rabbi would have anything to do with someone like Zacchaeus. Perhaps that is one of the reasons why they found Jesus difficult to accept.

There are few stories about Jesus coming into contact with Gentiles. But, on one occasion, he met a Roman centurion. He was a soldier, rather like a sergeant in today's army.

Read the story on page 35. It was probably intended to help Jews overcome their prejudice against the Romans. We call someone prejudiced if they dislike someone without any good reason.

▶ When Jesus entered Capernaum, a Roman officer met him and begged for help: 'Sir, my servant is sick in bed at home, unable to move and suffering terribly.'

'I will go and make him well,' Jesus said.

'Oh, no, sir,' answered the officer. 'I do not deserve to have you come into my house. Just give the order, and my servant will get well. I, too, am a man under the authority of superior officers, and I have soldiers under me. I order this one, "Go!" and he goes; I order that one, "Come!" and he comes; and I order my slave, "Do this!" and he does it.

When Jesus heard this he was surprised and said to the people following him, 'I tell you, I have never found anyone in Israel with faith like this.' . . .

Then Jesus said to the officer, 'Go home, and what you believe will be done for you.' And the officer's servant was healed that very moment.   Matthew 8:5–10, 13

Desmond Tutu has spent his life campaigning against apartheid. In 1984, he was awarded the Nobel peace prize. In 1986, he became Archbishop of Capetown, head of the Anglican Church in South Africa.

1 What is meant by (i) sinner; (ii) outcast; (iii) Gentile; (iv) prejudice?
2 a) Why did most Jews dislike tax-collectors?
b) Which words could be used to describe (i) Zacchaeus' reaction when Jesus told him he was coming to his house, (ii) the crowd's reaction?
c) How did Jesus affect Zacchaeus' life?
3 a) Why was Jesus surprised at the Roman officer?
b) Why might Jews have been surprised at what Jesus did?
4 a) Make a list of people who suffer today as a result of prejudice.
b) Read this page. Which of these people are prejudiced? Give reasons for your choices.
c) Suggest what could be done to overcome these prejudices. As a group, discuss your answers.

16 *The Parables*

Jesus used all kinds of methods in his teaching, just like your teachers. Sometimes he would talk to the people; at other times, he would do things to show them what he meant; often, he told them stories.

These were not ordinary stories; they were stories which had a meaning. They are known as **parables**. Other religious teachers also told parables, but Jesus seems to have used them more than most.

His parables do seem to have caught the attention of his listeners. Many of them were quite short and about everyday things which people could see around them.

Many of the parables were about the Kingdom of Heaven. Christians have different ideas about what this is. However, one way to understand it is to say that the Kingdom of Heaven will exist when people do what they believe God wants them to do.

Because no one has seen God, Jesus tried to compare him with real people. 'What's God like?' they would ask. And Jesus would reply, 'Well, he's like a shepherd. Let me tell you a story . . .' The shepherd is used as a symbol. He represents something which is difficult to explain.

Some of these stories were very simple to understand. He told listeners a story about a servant who owed a king a lot of money. Out of pity, the king let him off paying it. But the servant did not show the same pity to someone who owed him money. When the king heard about it, he put his servant in prison. He refused to let him out until he had paid everything he owed.

What has this got to do with God? Jesus was saying that, if God forgives people, they should forgive others. It was the same message he gave his disciples in the prayer he taught them.

You may know it as the Lord's Prayer. In it, Jesus said, 'Forgive us our sins, as we forgive those who sin against us.' What he meant was simple. If people cannot forgive others, God will not forgive them.

▶ A teacher of the Law came up and tried to trap Jesus . . . he asked Jesus, 'Who is my neighbour?'

Jesus answered, 'There was once a man who was going down from Jerusalem to Jericho when robbers attacked him, stripped him, and beat him up, leaving him half dead.

'It so happened that a priest was going down that road; but when he saw the man, he walked on by, on the other side. In the same way, a **Levite** also came along, went over and looked at the man, and then walked on by, on the other side.

'But a **Samaritan** who was travelling that way came upon the man, and when he saw him, his heart was filled with pity. He went over to him, poured oil and wine on his wounds and bandaged them; then he put the man on his own animal and took him to an inn, where he took care of him.

The road to Jericho. Jesus referred to this in the parable of the Good Samaritan. Ruins of an old inn still stand beside this road.

'The next day, he took out two silver coins and gave them to the innkeeper. "Take care of him," he told the innkeeper, "and when I come back this way, I will pay you whatever else you spend on him."'

And Jesus [asked], 'In your opinion, which one of these three acted like a neighbour towards the man attacked by the robbers?'   Luke 10:25, 29–36

A Good Samaritan

Corrie ten Boom was a Dutch Christian. When the Germans invaded Holland in 1940, her family helped Jews to escape from them. Here she is asking her minister to protect a Jewish mother and baby.

▶ 'Would you be willing to take a Jewish mother and her baby into your home? They will certainly be arrested.'

Colour drained from the minister's face. 'Miss ten Boom! It's just not safe! Think of your father! And your sister – she's never been strong.'

I pulled back the cover from the baby's face. There was a long silence. The [minister] bent forward, his hand in spite of himself reaching for the tiny feet curled round the blanket. Then he straightened.

'No. Definitely not! We could not lose our lives for that Jewish child!'

Father held the baby close, his beard brushing its cheek. 'You say we could lose our lives for that child. I would consider that the greatest honour that could come to my family.'

                              Corrie ten Boom: The Hiding Place

(The Jewish family was later arrested and killed by the Germans. Corrie was the only member of her family to survive.)

▶ Monday January 19th
I have joined a group at school called the Good Samaritans. We go out into the community helping and stuff like that. We miss Maths on Monday afternoons.

Today we had a talk on the sort of things we will be doing. I have been put in the old age pensioners' group. Nigel has got a dead yukky job looking after kids in a playgroup. He is as sick as a parrot.

      Sue Townsend: The Secret Diary of Adrian Mole

The good Samaritan, as drawn by an Indian artist.

1 a) What is a parable?
   b) Why do you think Jesus used parables to teach people?
2 a) Write down at least three things which you think make a good teacher.
   b) Which one do you think is most important? Give reasons.
   c) Read Matthew 7:28–29. What reason does he give for Jesus' success?
3 a) Read the story of the Good Samaritan. What was Jesus trying to teach the man?
   b) Read Corrie ten Boom's story. Would Jesus have approved of what her family did? If so, explain why.
   c) Read the extract from The Secret Diary of Adrian Mole. Do you think Nigel was a Good Samaritan? Give reasons.
4 Discuss in groups what Jesus was trying to say in the following parables. Write down what you decide.
   a) The unjust servant (on page 36)
   b) The lost sheep (Luke 15:1–7)
   c) The fishing net (Matthew 13:47–50)
5 Make up your own modern parable. It can be about anything you wish, but it must have a message for people to learn. Either write it as a story or as a play.

17 Forgiveness

There was a Jewish saying which said, 'Do not let a man have anything to do with the wicked.' In other words, you should have nothing to do with **sinners**. So the Pharisees were always amazed that Jesus mixed with sinners.

Luke writes that one day a group of people gathered round Jesus. They had come to hear him talk. But the Pharisees were complaining. They could not understand how Jesus could welcome such people. So he told them a parable called 'the **Prodigal** Son', which is about a lost son. This is a modern version of it.

▶ A father had two sons called Joseph and Benjamin. He loved them both dearly. One day, the younger son, Benjamin, asked his father for a share of the property. After much thought, his father agreed.

Far away, he spent his money on parties, drink and gambling. Slowly, his money dwindled away. As it disappeared, so did his friends.

Left without money, in a strange town, the only job he could get was feeding pigs. He was lucky to get that because a **famine** had hit the country.

'This is mad,' he said to himself. 'I'll go home. Even the servants have food there. I'll ask father to forgive me and see if he'll give me a job as a servant.'

What Benjamin didn't know was that his father had been looking out for him every day since he left home.

One afternoon, he saw Benjamin coming over the hill. 'At last,' he said quietly to himself. 'Thank God.' He was so happy he ran out to meet his son. Filled with **emotion**, the father threw his arms round him and kissed him.

Benjamin suddenly felt very guilty. 'Father, don't,' he said. 'I do not deserve this. I've been wrong. I'm sorry.' But his father would not listen. 'Come on home, son,' he said.

At home, he dressed Benjamin in new clothes and sandals. And, to show everyone that he had forgiven his son, he gave him his own ring to wear. 'We're going to celebrate,' he said. So a great feast was prepared and everyone was invited.

Just then, Joseph came back from town. 'What's going on?' he asked a servant. 'Your brother's back, sir,' he said.

'What!' shouted Joseph. 'Why on earth has he come back? Hasn't he had enough already?'

His father heard his voice and came out to him. 'Come on in, Joe,' he said.

'I'm not coming in with him there. In all the time I've been with you, I've never once asked for anything. I have done as you have asked me and what have you given me? Nothing.

'But as soon as your beloved Ben comes home, nothing is too good for him. He's wasted half your money – or have you forgotten that? Doesn't that make any difference?'

'Joe, my dear son,' said his father, 'don't you know that I wouldn't be without you for anything. Surely you know that I love you. But Ben – it was as if he were dead. And now he's alive again. I thought I'd lost him forever, but he's come back to me.'

This picture of the story is from a chapel in Zimbabwe.

Forgiving

During the second world war, the Nazi leader Adolf Hitler imprisoned millions of his enemies. Some were put into labour camps. They were fed very little but forced to work until they died.

Millions more were murdered in special camps called concentration camps. Many were gassed; others were hung, shot or given fatal injections. Probably five and a half million Jewish men, women and children died in this way. The Nazis also killed other people they saw as their enemies.

One of these camps was called Ravensbruck. When British troops captured the camp in 1945, the soldiers saw many horrible sights. The strangest thing they found was a prayer written by a woman prisoner. This is what it said:

▶ O Lord, remember not only the men and women of good will but also those of ill will. Do not only remember all the suffering they have inflicted on us. Remember the fruits we brought, thanks to this suffering . . . When they come to judgement, let all the fruits that we have borne be their forgiveness.

Some young people wrote about life in these special camps. This is how one Jewish teenager described life inside. His name was Petr Fischl and he died in 1944.

▶ We got used to standing in line at 7 o'clock in the morning, at 12 noon and again at 7 o'clock in the evening. We stood in a long queue with a plate in our hand, into which they ladled a little warmed-up water with a salty or coffee flavour, or else they gave us a few potatoes.

We got used to sleeping without a bed, to saluting every uniform, not to walk on sidewalks. We got used to undeserved slaps, blows and executions. We got accustomed to seeing people die, to seeing piled up coffins full of corpses, to seeing the sick amidst dirt and filth and to seeing helpless doctors.

We got used to [the fact] that, from time to time, one thousand unhappy souls would come here and that, from time to time, another thousand unhappy souls would go away.

Many people feel that the Nazis' war crimes should not be forgotten. This photograph shows the Yad Vashem memorial in Israel. It is one of many memorials to those who died.

1 Look carefully at the picture on page 38. Write down what you think you can see at the numbered places.

2 a) Look at the list of words below. Write down those which describe the reactions of (i) Joseph and (ii) his father, when Benjamin came home:
angry; happy; annoyed; upset; glad; hurt; overjoyed; ashamed; jealous; hateful.
b) What can you learn about Joseph and his father from their reactions?
c) Put yourself in Joseph's place. What would your reaction have been? Give reasons for your answer.

3 a) Read this page. Why did the woman in her prayer want God to remember people of 'ill will'?
b) Why might this woman argue that people should not hate the Nazis for what they did?
c) What words might describe Petr Fischl's feelings?
d) Write down what the woman might say to comfort this teenager.

18 Man of Mysteries

Look at the old photograph above. It was taken in 1908 in Siberia, Northern Russia. You are looking at what is left of a forest. What do you think has happened? Perhaps this local newspaper account provides a clue:

▶ The peasants saw a body shining very brightly with a bluish-white light. It moved downwards for about ten minutes. The body was in the form of a cylinder.

When the shining body approached the ground, it seemed to be **pulverized.** In its place a huge cloud of black smoke was formed. A loud crash, like gunfire, was heard. All the buildings shook. At the same time, a forked tongue of flame broke through the cloud. The old women wept; everyone thought that the end of the world was approaching.

Even today, we cannot be sure what had happened. But scientists did discover that something had exploded eight kilometres above ground level, while it was still in the air.

So was it an atomic explosion? Perhaps. Other people say it might have been a black hole, or a damaged spaceship, or a comet. We cannot be sure. But we do know that, if it had come down twelve hours later, it could have wiped out New York city.

It is just one of the many strange things which have happened in the world. Some are even less easy to explain than the explosion in 1908.

We think of them as mysteries or puzzles. Some eventually get solved. Others still baffle us – and people go on searching for an answer. The Bible contains quite a few puzzling stories. Here are just two of them.

▶ As Jesus was coming near Jericho, there was a blind man sitting by the road, begging. When he heard the crowd passing by, he asked, 'What is this?'

'Jesus of Nazareth is passing by,' they told him.

He cried out, 'Jesus! Son of David! Take pity on me!'

So Jesus stopped and ordered the blind man to be brought to him . . . Jesus asked him, 'What do you want me to do for you?'

'Sir,' he answered, 'I want to see again.'

Jesus said to him, 'Then see! Your faith has made you well.'

At once he was able to see, and he followed Jesus, giving thanks to God. When the crowd saw it, they all praised God.

Luke 18:35–38, 40–43

▶ Suddenly a strong wind blew up, and the waves began to spill over into the boat, so that it was about to fill with water . . .

Jesus stood up and commanded the wind, 'Be quiet!' and he said to the waves, 'Be still!' The wind died down and there was a great calm.

But they [the disciples] were terribly afraid and said to one another, 'Who is this man? Even the wind and the waves obey him!'

Mark 4:37, 39, 41

Modern Christians have different views about these puzzling stories. Some believe that they happened just as the gospels say they did; others find some of the stories hard to accept.

John's Gospel used the word 'sign' to describe these puzzling stories. Think of a road sign. What does it do? It gives us information about the road we are on.

These strange events were like signs to people who saw them. They said things about Jesus and his special relationship with God.

They told them that Jesus was a person who cared about the sick – a person who could heal, using God's power. At the same time, he had amazing powers over natural forces. These puzzling events showed God's power working through Jesus.

This scene from the film *Jesus of Nazareth* shows Jesus healing a paralysed man. The story is told in Luke 5:17–26.

1 a) What is a puzzle?
  b) How do you start to solve a puzzle?
  c) Do people enjoy solving puzzles? Give reasons.
2 a) What do you think John meant when he described these events as 'signs?'
  b) What might Christians believe they can learn about Jesus from these events?

3 Use a double page in your book and draw the diagram below. Fill in the grid, using page 40. (For the last one, read Luke 4:31–36.)
4 a) In pairs, make a list of reasons why people might (i) believe or (ii) not believe them.
  b) As a group, discuss whether you believe in these puzzling stories.

Event	Place	Eye-Witness	Their reaction	Reason why it was puzzling
Healing a blind man	Jericho			
Calming the wind	—			
Healing man with the demon	Synagogue		Amazed	

19 *Puzzling Stories*

A detective's job is to find out the truth. So he or she looks carefully at what takes place. If they really cannot solve the mystery, they put it aside until more evidence had been found.

There are two different kinds of puzzling story on the next page. It might help to work out the puzzles in small groups, then you can listen to each other's ideas.

This picture shows you what one group made of the first story on page 43.

Carl: Well, I believe the Bible. It's God's word. After all, Jesus was God's Son. So he could do anything. He created the world, so why couldn't he have made the food that those people needed?

Lynda: My grandpa had a friend who was a vicar. He told grandpa that something like this once happened to him when he was living in Derby. There were lots of people out of work. So the vicar tried to help by giving out food parcels. Sometimes he had them round for a meal. One day they had hardly anything on the table, but they still said thank you to God for their food. To everyone's surprise, the food didn't run out! There was enough for everybody!

Jason: Oh, come on, Lynda, you're pulling our leg! He must have been having your grandpa on. Things like that don't happen in the twentieth century!

Sharon: Of course, Jesus did later say that he was the 'Bread of Life'. Just as bread can keep people alive, so Christians believe Jesus gives them life.

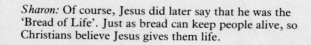

Wayne: I think there's a much easier way of understanding it. That little boy who gave Jesus the loaves and the fish made everybody think. Instead of being selfish, they decided to share their food. It's easy, when you think about it.

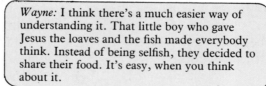

Narinder: I think the story is symbolic. It is trying to say that Jesus is the person who provides the disciples with all their daily needs. The bread and the fish stand for these needs.

► Jesus looked round and saw that a large crowd was coming to him, so he asked Philip, 'Where can we buy enough food to feed all the people?'

Philip answered, 'For everyone to have even a little, it would take more than 200 silver coins to buy enough bread.'

Another of his disciples, Andrew, . . . said, 'There is a boy here who has five loaves of barley bread and two fish. But they will certainly not be enough for all these people.'

'Make the people sit down,' Jesus told them. . . . So all the people sat down; there were about five thousand men. Jesus took the bread, gave thanks to God, and **distributed** it to the people who were sitting there. He did the same with the fish and they all had as much as they wanted.

When they were all full, he said to his disciples, 'Gather the pieces left over; let us not waste any'. So they gathered them all up and filled twelve baskets with the pieces left over . . .

Seeing this miracle that Jesus had performed, the people there said, 'Surely this is the Prophet, who was to come into the world.'

Jesus knew that they were about to come and seize him in order to make him king by force; so he went off again to the hills by himself.

John: 6:5, 7–15

A Modern Puzzle

Mary was captain of a Girls' Brigade company. For some time, she had been having problems with an ulcer on her right leg. Then, it grew much worse.

After much thought, she decided to go to a prayer meeting and ask for healing. At the meeting, a doctor from Durham examined her leg. **Pus** oozed from the front and the leg was badly swollen. Even if the ulcer cleared up, he said, it would need a skin graft.

During the meeting, the minister and his wife went across to Mary and prayed:

► 'Dear Father, just do your perfect will, as we trust you. In the name of Jesus Christ. Amen.'

When Mary removed the bandage the following morning to change the dressing there was a startling improvement. The whole area of destroyed flesh had grown over with the healthy pink of fresh tissue. The inflammation had gone. Only from a small sore spot at the front pus still oozed . . .

(A week later, the minister, with one of Mary's friends, prayed for her complete healing.)

Mary removed the bandage, and found that the healing was complete. It has remained so over the years. The following month, at the next prayer meeting, the Durham doctor declared, 'What has happened makes no kind of medical sense.'

D Phypers and D Bridges: *More Than Tongues Can Tell*

This painting is called *The Healing Presence*. It is at the entrance to the Christian Medical College Hospital at Vellore, India and was painted by a doctor.

1 What reasons are given for (i) believing and (ii) not believing the story of the loaves and fishes?

2 a) Give each of the children points out of ten for what they say. For instance, if you think Sharon has got it almost right, you could give her eight or nine marks.
b) Give reasons why you agree with the one which scored most marks.
c) Take the one which scored least marks. Explain why you gave it so few.

3 a) What did Narinder mean by saying it was 'symbolic'?
b) Do you agree that it doesn't really matter whether the story is true? Give reasons for your answer.

4 a) Read the story 'A Modern Puzzle'. How do you explain what happened to Mary?
b) Look back at the picture above. Who is the shadowy figure in the middle and what is he doing?
c) What do you think the painter was trying to say?

20 *The Last Week Begins*

This boy is riding through the streets on a donkey in memory of Jesus' own ride.

▶ A large crowd of people spread their cloaks on the road while others cut branches from the trees and spread them on the road.

The crowds walking in front of Jesus and those walking behind began to shout, 'Praise to David's Son! God bless him who comes in the name of the Lord! Praise God!'

When Jesus entered Jerusalem, the whole city was thrown into an uproar. 'Who is he?' the people asked.

'This is the prophet Jesus, from Nazareth in Galilee,' the crowds answered.

Matthew 21:8–11

Jesus' arrival in Jerusalem was certainly **spectacular.** It was also strange. Jerusalem was a holy city; pilgrims were expected to arrive on foot as a sign of respect. Even stranger, this is the only time in the gospels where Jesus is mentioned riding any sort of animal.

So why did he do it? Was it because, centuries earlier, according to the Old Testament, someone had said that the Messiah would arrive on a donkey?

The Jews who shouted, 'Praise to David's Son' obviously thought so. This is one of the titles used for the Messiah whom they expected.

But Jesus would have known it would cause quite a stir. He would have known, too, that he was a marked man from that moment onwards. The Sadducees would not accept it without a struggle.

▶ Jesus went into the Temple and drove out all those who were buying and selling there. He overturned the tables of the money-changers and the stools of those who sold pigeons, and said to them, 'It is written in the Scriptures that God said, "My Temple will be called a house of prayer." But you are making it a hideout for thieves!'
Matthew 21:12–13

His actions in the Temple would have made them even angrier. They were in charge of the Temple. That was why they asked him who had given him the right to interfere.

Some people believe that Jesus knew he was going to die – and that was why he had come to Jerusalem. But perhaps he just knew he was in danger. After all, he did not stay in the city at night; instead, he slept at Bethany, two miles away.

On just one night only, he did stay in the city. It was a Thursday. He planned to have supper with his disciples. It proved to be his last.

1 Write out the following events in the order in which they happened:
  a) Jesus teaches in the Temple.
  b) Jesus attacks the money-lenders' stalls
  c) The disciples find a donkey.
  d) People put their cloaks on the ground.
  e) Jesus rides into Jerusalem on a donkey.
2 How was Jesus' arrival different from that which the Jews expected of their King?
3 a) Do you think Jesus' followers would have been surprised by his behaviour in the Temple? Give reasons.
  b) Do you think he acted fairly? Again, give reasons.
4 Divide into groups. One half of your group should answer part (a); the other should answer part (b).
  a) You are a Sadducee who has seen Jesus' arrival. Write a report to the High Priest. In it, explain why you are unhappy at what you have seen.
  b) You are a follower of Jesus. Describe to a friend what you saw and how you felt when Jesus arrived.
  Then, compare the differences between your two versions.

21 The Last Supper

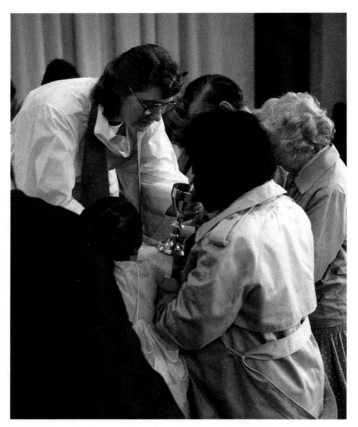

Holy Communion, the service which reminds Christians of the Last Supper.

Jerusalem would have been packed with people during that last week of Jesus' life. They had come for Passover. This festival reminded Jews of the time when their ancestors had escaped from Egypt, where they had been slaves. Jesus was in Jerusalem for the same reason.

Part of the festival involved a special meal. Two of the disciples got it ready; all twelve were present that night. They could hardly have expected what would happen next:

▶ While they were at the table eating, Jesus said, 'I tell you that one of you will betray me – one who is eating with me.'

The disciples were upset and began to ask him, one after the other, 'Surely you don't mean me, do you?'

Jesus answered, 'It will be one of you twelve, one who dips his bread in the dish with me.'

While they were eating, Jesus took a piece of bread, gave a prayer of thanks, broke it, and gave it to his disciples. 'Take it,' he said, 'this is my body.'

Then he took a cup, gave thanks to God, and handed it to them; and they all drank from it. Jesus said, 'This is my blood which is poured out for many' . . .

Mark 14:18–20, 22–24

▶ Then he took a piece of bread, gave thanks to God, broke it, and gave it to them, saying, 'This is my body, which is given for you. Do this in memory of me.'

Luke 22:19

Jesus was saying that the bread and wine were **symbols** – symbols of his body. His blood would be spilled and his body broken; in other words, he was going to die.

Washing the feet. This modern papercut is from China. (Notice the costumes.)

The Last Supper.

Soon afterwards, Luke tells us, an argument broke out among the disciples. They were arguing about which of them was the most important. Jesus had only just finished talking about his death, yet there they were, arguing about who would take over afterwards!

So Jesus told one last parable. In fact, he did more than tell it; he acted it. Taking a towel and a basin of water, he began to wash his disciples' feet. It was the sort of job a servant would do for guests.

He explained what it meant. His disciples were to follow his example and serve each other. No one should think he was more important than anyone else. Then, he gave his final instructions:

'As I have loved you, so you must love one another. If you have love for one another, then everyone will know that you are my disciples!'

The early Christian church believed this last supper was very important. What happened, and what Jesus said, had to be remembered. So they created a special service so that people would not forget.

The service is called Holy Communion. It is based on the events of the Last Supper. One young Christian explains why he takes part in it:

P	A	S	S	O	V	E	R	O	L
U	N	L	R	U	V	G	E	N	A
C	L	A	B	O	D	Y	E	R	S
Z	A	C	L	U	A	P	N	X	T
B	E	F	O	R	T	T	I	D	S
G	R	E	T	A	W	E	W	H	U
I	L	E	W	O	T	K	E	L	P
J	B	W	A	S	H	M	N	F	P
B	L	O	O	D	D	Q	U	R	E
P	E	L	P	I	C	S	I	D	R

1 This word search contains a number of words in this chapter. Write down each one that you find and beside each word, write a sentence about it.
2 Look at the lower photograph on page 46. What was Jesus trying to teach his disciples?
3 a) In groups discuss what the word 'love' means. Write down your ideas.
   b) What did Jesus mean by the word?
   c) Give four examples of ways in which Christians could follow this commandment to love one another.
   d) Give at least two ways in which they could go against it.
4 Suppose you were present at the Last Supper. Write a diary entry describing your feelings about what happened.
5 Make your own papercut of a scene during the last week of the life of Jesus.

22 *Betrayal*

Have you ever been let down by a friend? Perhaps they gave away a secret or talked about you behind your back. Maybe it hurt a little. You may even have felt you couldn't go on being their friend. You found you could not really trust them again.

Judas Iscariot, one of Jesus' closest friends, betrayed him. This is an imaginary account of an interview with one of the other apostles afterwards.

▶ 'Judas? I'd rather not talk about him.'
'Why?'
'Well, he was never really one of us. He came from Judea. I never knew why Jesus let him join us. Okay, so he looked after the money, but someone else could have done that.'
'But what did he do?'
'Don't you know? You must be the only person who doesn't! He **betrayed** Jesus. If it hadn't been for him, Jesus would still be alive today. Jesus said someone would betray him. It was at the last meal we had together, the night before he died. Just after Jesus said it, Judas left.'
'Didn't that make you suspicious?'
'No, silly really. I don't know why we didn't put two and two together at the time.'
'When did you work it out?'
'Later, in the Garden of Gethsemane. I still can't believe it. He brought along these Jewish soldiers, then went up to Jesus and kissed him. That was the sign to the soldiers. Then they arrested Jesus.'
'What happened to Judas?'
'Don't you know? He went off and hanged himself.'

Judas betrays Jesus.

▶ When Judas, the **traitor**, learnt that Jesus had been condemned, he **repented** and took back the thirty silver coins to the chief priests and the elders.
'I have sinned by betraying an innocent man to death!' he said.
'What do we care about that?' they answered. 'That is your business!'
Judas threw the coins down in the Temple and left; then he went off and hanged himself.

Matthew 27:3–5

Peter betrays Jesus.

Why did Judas betray Jesus? The gospels do not say and we will probably never know the answer. Perhaps he was just greedy and wanted the money.

But he may have wanted Jesus to prove he really was the Messiah. After all, Judas might have thought that Jesus would have to save himself if he was threatened with death. Then everyone would know he was the Messiah.

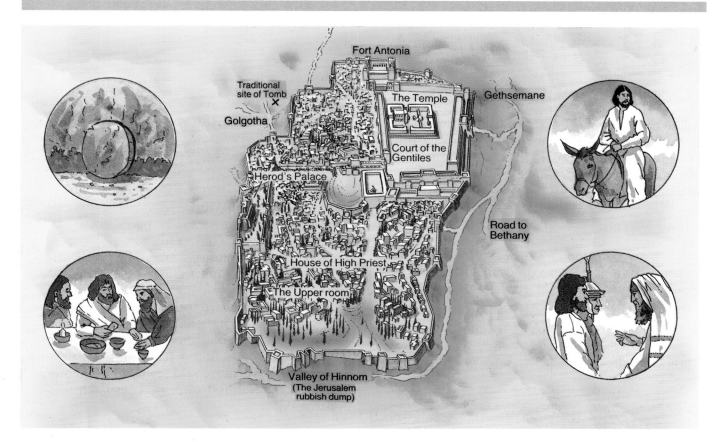

Map of Jerusalem in Jesus' time.

However, Judas was not the only disciple to let Jesus down. Most of them did, in one way or another. Matthew says, 'All the disciples left him and ran away'.

Even Peter, his right-hand man, let him down. Peter followed Jesus to the High Priest's house. In the courtyard, a servant girl questioned him twice. 'You were with Jesus,' she said.

Twice, he said that he had not been with him. Just at that moment, a cock crowed. Others in the yard may have noticed his accent. 'You cannot deny that you are one of them. You also come from Galilee.'

Peter became frightened: 'I swear that I am telling the truth. May God punish me if I am not! I do not know this man you are talking about.' Just then, a cock crowed for a second time.

Peter remembered what he had said while he was eating the Passover meal with Jesus: 'I will never leave you, even if the rest do. I will never deny you, even if I have to die.'

And Jesus replied, 'Before the cock crows twice, you will say three times that you do not know me.'

1 Copy out and complete this paragraph: Judas betrayed Jesus in the Garden of _____. He was paid _____ silver coins. Later, he was sorry for what he had done. He gave the coins back to the _____ _____ and killed himself.

2 a) Draw an outline map of Jerusalem.
b) What happened at (i) the Court of the Gentiles and (ii) Gethsemane?

3 a) Judas betrayed Jesus with a kiss. What is a kiss normally a symbol of?
b) What did Judas make it a symbol of?

4 a) Imagine you were a disciple. Who would you have thought easiest to forgive – Peter or Judas? Explain your answer in detail.
b) Describe an occasion when someone let you down.
c) Did you manage to forgive them or not? Explain why you did or didn't.

23 *On Trial*

After Jesus' arrest, he was taken to the High Priest's house. We do not know the exact time but it was probably early in the morning. None of his followers would have been around to object to his arrest.

Trial by the Sanhedrin

They tried various ways of finding him guilty of something, but they could not find enough evidence. Finally, the High Priest, Caiaphas, asked the key question:

▶ 'Are you the Messiah, the Son of the Blessed God?'

'I am,' answered Jesus, 'and you will all see the **Son of Man** seated on the right of the Almighty and coming with the clouds of heaven!'

The High priest tore his robes and said, 'We don't need any more **witnesses!** You heard his **blasphemy.** What is your decision?'

They all voted against him: he was guilty and should be put to death.

So, according to Mark, Jesus was found guilty of blasphemy. This meant he had spoken or acted as if he were God. This was a serious crime and people found guilty were stoned to death.

But the trial had not followed the normal Jewish rules:

- Trials at night were forbidden.
- Even Jewish writers have said that Jesus' words were not blasphemy.

However, they had found Jesus guilty. But only the Roman governor could sentence someone to death. So the **Sanhedrin** passed Jesus on to Pontius Pilate.

First Trial by Pontius Pilate

Early on Friday morning, the chief priests brought Jesus to Pilate. They now accused him of three things:

- Telling people not to pay their taxes.
- Claiming to be the Messiah, King of the Jews.
- Misleading the Jewish people.

So Pilate questioned Jesus. But he could not find him guilty on any of the charges which had been made against him. This made the priests angry. They then claimed that Jesus had been starting riots. Hearing this, Pilate decided to pass Jesus on to Herod Antipas. He was ruler of Galilee, where Jesus lived.

Trial by Herod Antipas

Herod got no further than Pilate had done, and simply sent Jesus straight back to him.

Second Trial by Pontius Pilate

Yet again, Pilate told the priests that Jesus was innocent. However, it seems there was a custom

Christ before the High Priest by Honthorst.

to release one prisoner as it was Passover time.

Whether Pilate gave the crowd a choice of prisoners is not clear. But the crowd wanted him to free a murderer called Barabbas. Some people think he may have been a Zealot.

Matthew records what happened next. Pilate got a bowl of water and washed his hands in front of the crowd. He told them, 'I am not responsible for the death of this man. This is your doing!'

Jesus' fate was sealed.

This Mexican is taking part in a Good Friday procession. His crown of thorns reminds people of the one which Jesus wore. (See John 19:1–2.)

Why was Jesus condemned?

Theory 1: there was a plot

▶ So the Pharisees and the chief priests met with the **Council** and said, 'What shall we do? Look at all the miracles this man is performing! If we let him go on this way, everyone will believe in him, and the Roman authorities will take action and destroy our Temple and our nation!'

...Caiaphas, who was High Priest that year, said, 'What fools you are! Don't you realize that it is better for you to let one man die for the people, instead of having the whole nation destroyed?'...

From that day on the Jewish authorities made plans to kill Jesus. So Jesus did not travel openly in Judea, but left and went to a place near the desert...

John 11:47–50; 53–54

Theory 2: he was a sorcerer

▶ Yeshu practised **sorcery** and led astray Israel.

Talmud

This is the only piece of evidence from outside the Bible. Sorcery is the practice of black magic. But the punishment for this was being stoned to death – and Jesus was not stoned to death.

The Jewish authorities may have been afraid that Jesus was going to proclaim himself king. If people believed he was the Messiah, they might have joined him. There might be a revolt against the Romans. Then, the Romans would crush it and all Jews might suffer.

Theory 3: he was the 'Lamb of God'

▶ John the Baptist called Jesus the 'Lamb of God'. At Passover, Jewish people sacrificed a lamb. It reminded them that they had been freed from slavery in Egypt.

In the same way, Christians believe that Jesus' sacrifice gave them freedom. His death freed Christians from God's punishment for their sin. If it is not forgiven, a person is separated from God forever.

1 Match up the name on the left with the description on the right.

Pilate	the convicted murderer
Caiaphas	the ruler of Galilee
Herod Antipas	the Roman governor
Barabbas	the High Priest

2 a) Describe the part which each man in question 1 played in the trials of Jesus.
b) Which charge against Jesus was most important for (i) Caiaphas and (ii) Pontius Pilate? Explain how you decided.

3 a) Which of the following people do you think was responsible for Jesus being put to death: Pontius Pilate; Caiaphas; the Roman Emperor; the Sanhedrin; Barabbas; Herod Antipas? Give a reason for each choice you make.
b) Who else, if anyone, was responsible? Give reasons for any choice you make.

4 a) If the disciples ran away, how do we know about the trials?
b) Are these accounts likely to be accurate? Give a reason.
c) Would the disciples' accounts have been more accurate? Explain your answer.

24 *Death by Crucifixion*

Many people think there was something unusual about the way Jesus died. But **crucifixion** was a common punishment in Roman times. It was normally used for non-Romans who were murderers or traitors. After one revolt in the first century BCE, nearly 6500 people were put to death in this way.

Early Christians would not use the cross as their holy symbol. They held the Jewish belief about people executed on a cross. In their **Torah** it is said that anyone hung on a tree was cursed by God. For them, Jesus was hung (crucified) on a tree (the cross).

Jesus was **flogged** before setting out for the crucifixion. Three gospels say a bystander carried his cross; one gospel says he carried it himself. Probably, Jesus carried the crosspiece only. It would have weighed up to 56 kilograms.

He walked the 700 metres to Golgotha, where criminals were usually put to death. Once there, he was offered a drink which probably contained drugs. He refused it.

The 'Street of Sorrows' in modern Jerusalem. It is believed that Jesus passed through here on his way to Golgotha.

No one is sure exactly where Golgotha was. This rocky area is one possibility. Do you think it looks like a skull?

How long it took a crucified person to die depends on how the Romans did it. A crucifixion was not always the same every time. It could be made longer by fixing a kind of seat to the cross; it could be made shorter by smashing the legs of the dying man. It could take anything from thirty minutes to three days. Eventually, the victim **suffocated.**

Jesus lasted from nine o'clock on Friday morning until three o'clock in the afternoon. At the end, a soldier offered him a sponge soaked in wine, vinegar, water and beaten eggs. Jesus drank from it and said, 'It is finished.'

John's Gospel says the Roman soldiers were surprised to find him dead. To make sure, they stabbed his side with a spear. Blood and water dripped from the wound. It was a sign that his heart had collapsed. He was dead.

Evidence outside the Bible for Jesus' death.

▶ Christus had been executed in the reign of Tiberius by the **procurator** Pontius Pilate.

Tacitus (c.CE 116)

▶ Pilate, at the suggestion of the principal men amongst us, condemned him to the cross.

Josephus (CE 94)

▶ On the eve of Passover they hanged Yeshu of Nazareth.

The Talmud (5th century)

▶ When Jesus came to Golgotha
  they hanged him on a tree,
They drove great nails through hands and feet,
  and made a Calvary;
They crowned him with a crown of thorns,
  red were his wounds and deep,
For those were crude and cruel days,
  and human flesh was cheap.

When Jesus came to Birmingham
  they simply passed him by,
They never hurt a hair of him,
  they only let him die;
For men had grown more tender,
  and they would not give him pain.
They only just passed down the street,
  and left him in the rain.

Still Jesus cried, 'Forgive them,
  for they know not what they do,'
And still it rained the wintry rain
  that drenched him through and through;
The crowds went home and left the streets
  without a soul to see,
And Jesus crouched against a wall
  and cried for Calvary.   G A Studdert-Kennedy

1 Copy out and complete this paragraph:
  Jesus was flogged before his crucifixion at
  _____ o'clock at a place called _____.
  He died after about _____ hours, at
  _____ o'clock.
2 Read the parts of the Bible in brackets to
  find the answers.
  a) What was the attitude of these people
  to Jesus: the chief priests (Matthew
  27:41–43); the Roman soldiers (Luke
  23:36–37, 47 and Mark 15:24)?
  b) What was Jesus' attitude towards these
  people: his executioners (Luke 23:34); his
  mother (John 19:25–27); the repentant
  thief (Luke 23:39–43); God his Father
  (Mark 15:34 and Luke 23:46)?
3 Read the poem opposite. How have
  people's attitudes towards Jesus changed?
4 Imagine you are one of the people present
  at the crucifixion. Write a poem to show
  your feelings and thoughts about the
  event.

Nails (or a nail) were driven
through the heel bone.
The one found measured
17 centimetres.

The victim carried the cross-beam to the execution-ground.

It is likely that the cross
was T-shaped.

Nails were driven through
the wrists to support the
body.

Clothing was removed
by soldiers.

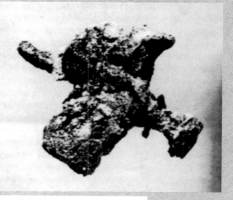

Leg bones were smashed to
speed up death. This meant
the lungs filled with fluid and
the man suffocated.

Unlike this man, Jesus' legs
were not broken. The notice
THE KING OF THE JEWS was
placed above Jesus' head.

This crucifix is a symbol of
Christ's death on the cross.
Many churches have a cross
on the altar as a symbol that
Jesus has risen. It reminds
Christians of their belief that
Jesus defeated death.

Artists and the Crucifixion

The birth and death of Jesus have inspired artists for well over a thousand years. Wherever there are Christians, you will find paintings and drawings of these events.

The selection on these pages has been drawn from many different lands. Each shows how one Christian imagines this key event in their faith. As you look at them, try to work out, too, what the artist felt about the event.

B: On the way to the execution (Senegal).

A: Images of the crucifixion in a stained glass window.

C: A statue of Christ in Palma.

D: A black Christ shown on the wall of a church in Africa.

E: A woodcut by the German artist Durer.

1 a) Which of these pictures do not show Christ on the cross?
b) Which details in pictures B and E fit the account in the Bible?
2 a) Which details are *wrong* in picture E?
b) Which crucifixion scene is closest to the drawing on page 53? Explain how you decided.
3 a) In which pictures is Christ shown as black? Suggest a reason for this.
b) Why do you think he is shown as white in pictures C and E?
4 Draw your own picture of any one part of the crucifixion story. (It does not have to be the execution itself.)

26 Two Mysteries and One Solution

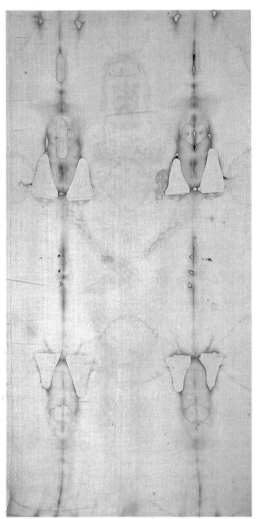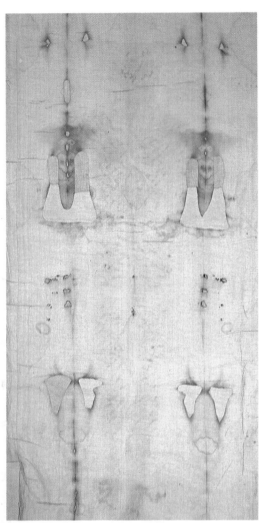

Above: (left) front view of Turin Shroud; (right) Back view of Turin Shroud.

In the cathedral at Turin in Italy is a remarkable object. It does not look all that special; it is a strip of yellowing cloth, over a metre wide and over four metres long.

They call it the Holy Shroud. A shroud is the cloth in which a dead person is buried. For centuries, many people believed that this shroud was the one used to bury Jesus.

Photographs of it showed a man with wounds like Jesus would have had. There seemed to be bloodstains from a crown of thorns and back wounds caused by whipping.

In 1988, scientists in three cities used tests, known as carbon dating, on the cloth. These showed that the shroud was almost certainly made between 1260 and 1390 CE. If so, it cannot be Jesus' shroud.

However, the tests have raised new questions. How was the fake made? The shroud clearly shows a man who had been crucified. But crucifixion was banned centuries earlier.

No painter of the time is known to have the skill to create such a realistic figure. Anyway, X-rays have shown there are no brush marks.

Some experts think the cloth may have been wrapped round a life-size statue of Jesus which had been heated.

The Catholic Church had never claimed that the shroud was genuine and so it will probably remain in Turin Cathedral. One adviser to the Bishop of Turin said, 'Now it is an even more mysterious relic.'

Equally mysterious are people who have stigmata on their body. Stigmata are the marks of Christ's crucifixion. In the 20th century, the most famous such person was Padre Pio, an Italian priest. His wounds first appeared in 1918. They remained with him until his death fifty years later.

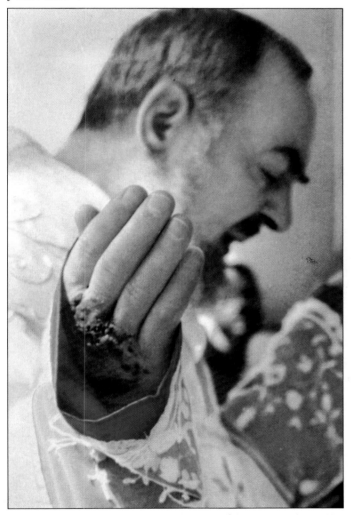

Because he bled from the palms of his hands, he wore mittens to hide them. But, before mass, he took these off. Michael Buckley helped Padre Pio for a while. He described what he saw:

▶ I was kneeling behind him and so his hand was between me and the candle. When he lifted up his hands to pray, you could see the light of the candle through his hands as if it was filled with blood.

Doctors could not explain Padre Pio's wounds. Oddly, after he died in 1968, there was hardly a trace of the wounds on his hands. His feet had completely healed.

What is strange about people with stigmata is that they bleed through the palms of their hands. Yet Romans crucified people with nails through the wrists.

Claretta Robertson is a Baptist. Her stigmata first appeared when she was ten:

▶ I've often wondered – why me? There are a lot of people who don't believe that there's a God or Jesus. I think he did it to show people there is a God.

Some people think that stigmata are caused by the mind. People feel so strongly about Jesus' suffering that they bleed in sympathy. If that is true, they show the remarkable power of religious faith.

---

1 Suppose you believed the shroud was genuine. Then, you discovered that tests showed it was not. Which of the following words would describe your feelings?
(i) sad; (ii) relieved; (iii) depressed; (iv) lonely; (v) not bothered; (vi) happy; (vii) angry; (viii) peaceful; (ix) hopeful. Give reasons for your answers.

2 a) Why do you think many people wanted to believe it was genuine?
b) Why did the bishop's adviser say it was 'now even more mysterious'?

3 a) What are stigmata?
b) What three main wounds would you expect these people to have?

4 a) In groups, write down as many explanations as you can for these wounds appearing.
b) You are journalists sent to interview Claretta Robertson. Write down five questions you would want to ask her.
c) As a class, compare your answers to (a) and (b).

27 *The Resurrection*

One of a Christian's key beliefs is that Jesus came back to life after he died. It is called the resurrection. The apostles all believed it. There is, however, only one piece of evidence for this from outside the Bible.

► He appeared to them alive on the third day as the prophets had foretold.   Josephus, 'Antiquities'

However, no one is sure that this sentence is genuine. It could have been added later by a Christian. So all we really have are the four versions in the gospels. The problem is that they do not always seem to agree.

THE WOMEN WENT TO THE WRONG TOMB...

JESUS WAS **NOT REALLY DEAD**. PERHAPS THE LAST DRINK WAS DRUGGED TO MAKE HIM APPEAR DEAD...

JESUS HAD BEEN BURIED SOMEWHERE ELSE BY THE ROMANS...

JESUS DID NOT RISE FROM THE DEAD SO THE DISCIPLES TOOK THE BODY TO MAKE IT LOOK AS IF HE HAD...

PEOPLE HAD HALLUCINATIONS. THEY WANTED TO THINK HE WAS ALIVE, SO THEY IMAGINED IT...

THE ROMANS TOOK IT AWAY AND PERHAPS BURNED IT...

THE BODY WAS STILL THERE BUT THEY FELT HIS PRESENCE WITH THEM...

JESUS HAD RISEN FROM THE DEAD...

No one knows what happened to the body after Jesus was put in the tomb. These pictures show you some ideas people have had.

A rock tomb with the stone rolled back from the entrance.

This altar cross in Namibia showing the crucified Christ is a symbol that Jesus has risen. It reminds Christians of their belief that Jesus defeated death.

However, one person features in each gospel story. She is Mary Magdalene, who was a disciple of Jesus. Here is a modern account of her story, based on what the New Testament tells us.

► Can I forget that Sunday morning? It's burnt deep into my memory. I remember my friend, Mary, and I were so sad. We hadn't slept at all since the day Jesus died. We couldn't understand why it happened. He was such a good man.

Anyway, we decided to go to his tomb. You see, he'd been buried in such a hurry. We wanted to take some oils to **anoint** him.

We didn't hurry. We were worrying about that stone. It was so large. We didn't know how we'd be able to move it. But we needn't have worried. The stone wasn't there!

We didn't know what to think. We were excited and frightened at the same time. We went into the tomb. This next bit is going to sound silly.

I think there was a man sitting inside, dressed in white. Mary said afterwards that he was an angel. Who knows? Perhaps he was.

Anyway, he said, 'Don't be afraid. He's not here. He's gone to Galilee, just as he said he was going to.' And I glanced down at the ledge where his body should have been. It wasn't there!

Well, I was shaking, I can tell you. We got out of that tomb as fast as we could. But we hadn't got very far when . . .

But you won't believe this. We saw Jesus, just as clearly as I can see you now. He told us not to be afraid and gave us a message for his friends, just like the angel said.

So Mary went to find the disciples. Not one of them believed her. They thought she had imagined it all. But they soon found out they were wrong.

1 a) Read Mary Magdalene's story. Write down those words which describe her feelings.
b) Write the diary entry which Mary Magdalene might have made the night after she sees Jesus again.
2 a) Look at the drawings opposite. Take each suggestion in turn and give it a mark out of ten. For instance, if you think the first is very unlikely, you might only give it 2 out of 10.
b) Think about the idea to which you gave the highest marks. Give reasons why it is your top choice.
3 Design a symbol which Christians could use for Jesus' resurrection. (Do not use a cross.) Then, explain how you made your choice.

28 The Risen Christ

According to Luke, it was not until forty days after the resurrection that Jesus 'disappeared from their sight'. This event is called the **Ascension**. Christians believe this means that Jesus returned to God.

But before he left, he gave his disciples some instructions. He told them to:

- return to Jerusalem and wait for the Holy Spirit. Then they could:
- preach the gospel and
- baptise those who believed their message.

Ten days afterwards, some strange events took place. Modern Christians call this day *Whitsun*. The story on this page is a modern version of what happened, based on chapter two of the Acts of the Apostles. It is told by an ordinary person who might have been present.

A stained-glass window at Westminster Abbey, London.

▶ Early in the morning, just before nine o'clock, we were startled by a strange noise. It sounded like a very strong wind.

Soon afterwards, some of the followers of Jesus of Nazareth turned up. Nobody had heard much from them since their Master's death. I suppose they didn't want to share his fate.

These disciples began to speak to the crowd. It was strange. There were people from all over the world, but everyone knew exactly what they were saying. Some of the crowd couldn't make it out. 'You're drunk!' they shouted.

And then Peter stood up. You couldn't fail to recognise him; he was a big, burly fellow. I was told he'd denied knowing Jesus the night before the crucifixion. Well, he didn't mind admitting he knew him that day!

Peter told us that God had given all of them his Spirit. That was why everyone could hear them speak in their own language. It was one of God's gifts to them.

He told us all that Jesus had been brought back to life by God. He claimed that all the disciples had seen him. Jesus was the one some of us had hoped would free us from Roman rule. But I didn't see how he could have been the Messiah. I mean, God wouldn't have let him get killed, would he?

Anyway, lots of people started shouting out, 'What shall we do?' Peter told them to repent and be baptised. It was rather like hearing John the Baptist again.

Well, I heard that three thousand people believed what the fishermen said. They were baptised and became followers of this Jesus. I don't know what to make of it!

How can you follow a dead man?

Badges worn by today's young Christians.

> ► He lives, he lives,
> Christ Jesus lives today!
> He walks with me and talks with me
> Along life's narrow way.
> He lives, he lives,
> **Salvation** to impart!
> You ask me how I know he lives?
> He lives within my heart.   A H Ackley 1983

Perhaps these Christians do not dress as you might expect them to. One young Christian said, 'Jesus doesn't care about what people wear. He looks right through that'. Do you agree?

In 1943, Catherine Marshall was suffering from a serious disease; she had become very weak. She had asked God to heal her but nothing happened until September 14 . . .

► I woke up at 3.30 a.m. It was pitch black, not a sound. I don't know why I woke up, but suddenly I became aware of a **presence** in the room. I could see nothing, but somehow I knew that a person was standing by the right-hand side of my bed. He seemed so loving. He smiled at me.

'Why do you take your problems so seriously? Relax! There's nothing here I can't take care of.' I suddenly realised he knew all about me, every detail of my life.

'Go and tell your mother,' he said. And then he smiled again. 'That's simple enough, isn't it?'

'Go and tell my mother what?' I thought. 'It's the middle of the night. What will she think?' I **wavered** between disobeying him and doing what I knew was right. 'I'll do it if it kills me,' I told him as I threw off the bed covers. He smiled again and stood aside for me to pass . . .

A few minutes later, when I returned to my bedroom, it was empty. I lay awake until dawn, amazed at what had happened. I had been in the presence of Christ.

I understood now why not even the threat of death could shake Peter, James and John from their belief that Jesus was alive. How was his resurrection possible? I had no idea. But suddenly all the arguments seemed unimportant in the face of the fact that it was true.

Catherine Marshall: *Beyond Ourselves*

(Afterwards, she began to get better.)

Not all Christians have the kind of experience that Catherine Marshall did. But they all believe Jesus is alive today; he is as real for them as the person sitting next to you is for you.

1 Draw the word puzzle below. Make up your own clues to fit these answers. You could hold a class competition to see who can come up with the best clue to the word reading downwards!
  a)   P R E S E N C E
  b) R I S E N
  c) W H I T S U N
  d) A S C E N S I O N
  e) S P I R I T
2 Read the story on page 60. Suppose you were the author. Write a letter to a friend.
Explain why you find it hard to believe Jesus was the Messiah.
3 a) Peter was a changed man after the resurrection. Explain what this means.
  b) Give two reasons which may have caused this change.
4 a) How did Catherine Marshall know she had met Jesus that night?
  b) How did it affect her?
  c) Write a conversation between Catherine and her mother, when Catherine tries to explain what happened.

Connections

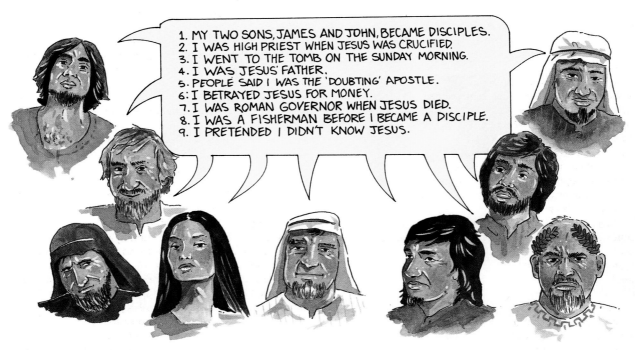

1. MY TWO SONS, JAMES AND JOHN, BECAME DISCIPLES.
2. I WAS HIGH PRIEST WHEN JESUS WAS CRUCIFIED.
3. I WENT TO THE TOMB ON THE SUNDAY MORNING.
4. I WAS JESUS' FATHER.
5. PEOPLE SAID I WAS THE 'DOUBTING' APOSTLE.
6. I BETRAYED JESUS FOR MONEY.
7. I WAS ROMAN GOVERNOR WHEN JESUS DIED.
8. I WAS A FISHERMAN BEFORE I BECAME A DISCIPLE.
9. I PRETENDED I DIDN'T KNOW JESUS.

1 **Who said what?**

Draw the grid below in your exercise book, using a pencil and ruler. Next, look at what the people above are saying. Your job is to work out who said what. For example, if you think Joseph would have said 'I was a fisherman before I became a disciple', put a tick beside Joseph in box 8. But be careful. There are more people in the list than in the drawing!

	1	2	3	4	5	6	7	8	9
Joseph									
Judas Iscariot									
Peter									
Mary Magdalene									
Barabbas									
Luke									
Mary									
Pontius Pilate									
Caiaphas									
Mark									
Thomas									
Zebedee									

2 There were no newspapers in Jesus' time. If there had been, here are four headlines you might have read:

(i) FOOD FOR EVERYONE: FIVE THOUSAND FED.
(ii) STAR GUIDES WISE MEN TO BABY'S BIRTHPLACE.
(iii) DESERT WILD MAN BAPTISES PEOPLE IN RIVER JORDAN.
(iv) WILD SCENES DURING DONKEY RIDE THROUGH CITY STREETS.

a) Explain briefly what each headline is about.
b) Choose any event from Jesus' life and write your own news story about it. You could make a group newspaper by adding other news stories and making up suitable advertisements and pictures.

3 Early Christians used the fish as a symbol of Jesus; later ones used a cross. Think of your own symbol for the *birth* of Jesus and draw it carefully in your book. Then, explain in detail how you decided on it.

Glossary

anoint – put oil on

apartheid – system of keeping whites and blacks separate

apostle – one of the twelve men chosen by Jesus to preach the gospel

Ascension – Jesus' going up to heaven

authority – power or person who has power

baptised – dipped into water as a sign of washing away sin

betrayed – let down; deceived

biased – favouring one side too much

blasphemy – words spoken against God

catacombs – underground burial places

census – official count of a country's population

congregation – people who have come together to worship

convent – building where women live who devote themselves to religion

council – small group of people chosen to make laws

crucifixion – method of killing people by nailing them to crosses

disciple – follower (of Jesus)

distributed – shared round

emotion – strong feeling

famine – lack of food

flogged – beaten or whipped

hallucinations – things seen or heard which do not exist

Levite – temple assistant to the priests

loyal – faithful

Messiah – person the Jews expected to save them

missionary – person who travels to persuade people to join a religion

mosaic – picture made from pieces of stone

New Testament – the part of the Bible which is about Jesus and his life

notify – inform

nonconformist – person who refuses to conform to rules

nun – woman who gives up everything for religion

outcasts – people thrown out of society

pagan – not Christian

papyrus – kind of paper made from water plants

parable – short story which has a lesson to teach

paralysed – crippled

persecuted – hunted down and made to suffer

Pharisees – Jews who strictly obeyed religious laws

prayer – act of speaking to God

presence – something, or somebody, present

primary sources – a piece of writing or a picture written or drawn at the time of the event being studied

procurator – person in charge of an area

prodigal – wasteful

prophet – person who speaks on behalf of God

pulverized – ground down to powder

pus – thick liquid found in sores

repented – asked to be forgiven

Sabbath – Jewish day of rest and worship

sacrifice – something killed as an offering to a god

Sadducee – important Jewish priest

salvation – saving the soul by freeing from sin

Samaritan – someone who lives in Samaria. Now used to describe a person who helps someone in trouble

Sanhedrin – Jewish council

scripture – holy writing

sinner – a person who does and thinks things which offend God

Son of Man – title used by gospel writers to describe Jesus

sorcery – witchcraft

spectacular – making a great display

suffocated – choked to death

symbol – something which stands for or represents something else

synagogue – building used for worship by Jews

tax-collector – person who collects taxes (money taken from people by their rulers)

Torah – name used by Jews for the first five books of their scripture

traitor – person who betrays somebody or something

underground movement – secret organisation

wavered – could not make up one's mind

witnesses – people who saw something happen

worship – service in honour of God; great honour and respect

Zealot – member of a Jewish sect resisting the Romans

Index